KEYSTONE OF THE TAROT WITH MEDITATIONS

THE HOLY ORDER OF MANS

Holy Order of MANS
Corte Madera, California

Copyright © 2012 Holy Order of MANS All Rights Reserved
Published by Holy Order of MANS, Corte Madera, CA
holyorderofmans.org

No parts of this book may be reproduced in any form or by any electronic or mechanical means, including information retrieval systems, without prior written permission from the author.

Cover and interior layout and design by Carolyn Oakley,
Luminous Moon Design + Press, Boulder, Colorado
luminousmoon.com

First Edition
Second Printing: August 2022

ISBN-13: 978-1-7370176-7-7

Body, Mind & Spirit: Divination: Tarot — Body, Mind & Spirit: Astrology — Body, Mind & Spirit: Mysticism

Printed and bound in the United States of America

Other Publications by Holy Orders of MANS

The Golden Force
Tarot 22 Keys – The Major Arcana (tarot card set)

Forthcoming

Jewels of the Wise: Self-Mastery Through the Tarot
Stars of Heaven: Mystical Astrology

DEDICATION

*To those who wish to transform their lives through the
Wisdom of the Ages, welcome!*

Keystone of the Tarot with Meditations

Acknowledgments

Keystone of the Tarot and *Tarot Meditations* were originally published as separate volumes by the Holy Order of MANS in 1967. These two books are now combined into one volume titled *Keystone of the Tarot with Meditations*. By the late 1980's, the Holy Order of MANS came apart and, consequently, their books were no longer available. Special thanks to Mark and Mary Anderson of the Science of Man who created a website in the 1990's and made these Order books available online. Special thanks also to those who continued to do the Work of the Order during this time; and to Mary Ray who took on the daunting task of retyping most of the Order literature, including these books, in the mid 1990's and putting it on the website HolyOrderOfMANS.org. Special thanks to Margot Whitney, Director, Holy Order of MANS who, in 2012, resurrected the Holy Order of MANS for the 21st Century. Thank you to Carolyn Oakley at Luminous Moon Design for her patience and talented work designing and laying out the book and cover. And thank you to Michael Maciel, Director, Holy Order of MANS, for his contributions toward the publication of this book.

Most importantly, and with heartfelt gratitude, we placed our trust in God.

"…and Jesus looking upon them saith, 'With men it is impossible, but not with God; for with God all things are possible.' " (Mark 10:27)

Keystone of the Tarot with Meditations

INTRODUCTION

Keystone of the Tarot with Meditations is designed for you to use as an instruction manual for your personal deck of Tarot cards, *Tarot 22 Keys – The Major Arcana*, available from Holy Order of MANS. It is a concise explanation of the symbology of Tarot in a nutshell.

Coloring instructions for the Major Arcana are included. Brief and clear explanations of the symbols are given in order for you to recognize and understand the symbolism when you see it in your life and the world around you.

The 32 Paths of Wisdom are presented in their true spiritual context so that you can see for yourself the relationship between the teachings of the ancients and the Tarot.

Meditation on the symbols in their proper sequence will reveal a great deal to the student who will take a few minutes each day, beginning with The Fool and progressing through the entire deck. The statements relating to each card are worded simply so that they may be easily used in meditation. Better results can be obtained if you are also coloring, or have colored, the corresponding cards and look at them before starting to meditate.

The meditations offered in this book are the inspirations of a Christian mystic and spiritual teacher, Rt. Rev. Helen Blighton, who studied and contemplated the Tarot and Cabalistic Tree of Life for many years.

Blighton, with her husband Rt. Rev. Earl W. Blighton, created the Science of Man in June 1961, and the Holy Order of MANS, as a seminary, in July 1968. The Holy Order of MANS was incorporated once again in February 2012 to continue their work.

Known as Mother Ruth within the Order, she developed a series of lessons for students of these ancient wisdom teachings. They are published in the books *Jewels of the Wise: Self-Mastery Through the Tarot*, *Keystone of the Tarot with Meditations*, *Stars of Heaven: Mystical Astrology*, and *Tarot 22 Keys – The Major Arcana* (Tarot card set).

Tarot 22 Keys – The Major Arcana cards offered by the Holy Order of MANS were carefully designed and inspired as a result of Mother Ruth's meditation. Mindful of the profound symbology contained in each Key, she was respectful of the contributions of Paul Foster Case, Jason Lotterhand, and many other teachers who carried forward the mystical tradition of the Tarot as the Path of Initiation, and the workings of mind and soul on the Way to enlightenment.

Mother Ruth's influence, strength and power uplifted the hearts of all that came into her presence and were touched by her writing. The garden she planted here on earth will continue to grow far beyond our time.

Writing about the 22 Keys she said, "Even the minute features of each picture, as many students know, carry amazing revelations of truth, which unfold not all at once, nor even on the first time around in study, but gradually over a period of time in accordance with the attention given."

A meditation is given for each of the 22 Keys of the Major Arcana to draw the student into a more in-depth vision of what each key represents. One should use them as a complement to the lessons and coloring of the Keys.

May the beauty of your inner life blossom as you engage in the Great Quest.

The Holy Order of MANS is an organization dedicated to a more thorough understanding of the universal laws of the Creator, so that all might better manifest God's Creation and thus promote Peace and Harmony among people everywhere. Our purpose is to teach the Ancient Christian wisdom to this new generation as it was taught in the past.

Our organization is called the Holy Order of MANS because the universal laws of creation, the law of prayer, and other principles can be taught and, in your everyday life, you can become the master of your fate through conscious application of these principles.

We use the term "man" to include both men and women.

Keystone of the Tarot with Meditations

Contents

Dedication v

Acknowledgments vii

Introduction ix

Holy Order of MANS xi

Thirty-Two Paths of Wisdom 15

The Ten Spheres of Emanation on the Tree of Life 19

Coloring the Ten Spheres on the Tree of Life 23

The 78 Cards in the Tarot Deck 27

Coloring the Major Arcana Tarot Keys 29

The Twenty-Two Keys (0-21) with Symbology,
Coloring Instructions and Meditations 35

The Tarot Tableau as a Lightning Flash 171

Illustrations

Tree of Life 14

32 Paths of Wisdom on the Tree of Life (chart) 18

The Tarot Tableau 170

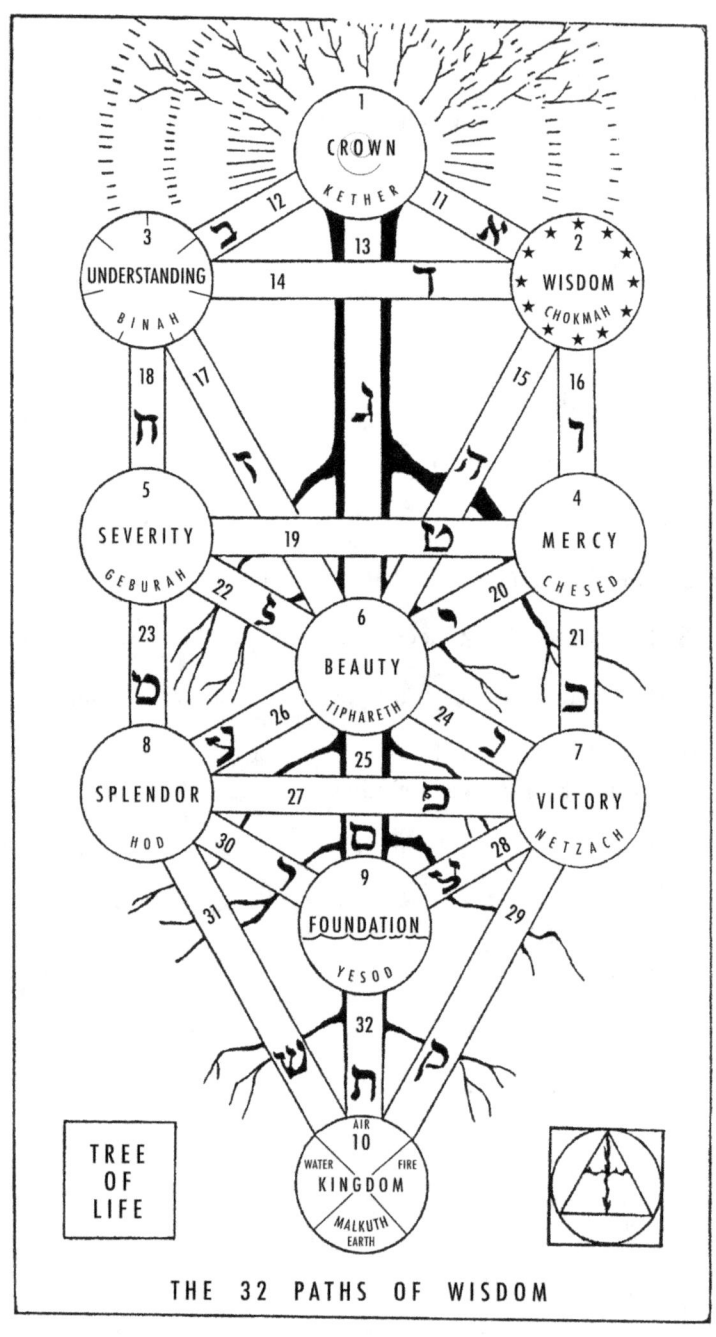

Thirty-Two Paths of Wisdom

"There are many Paths, but all lead into One Way."

God is essentially without form, but in His manifestation, He is seen or discerned under different aspects, according to a scale of degrees which unfold in studying the Paths of Wisdom. The ancient Cabala states that the most secret of all Mysteries is that which is called No Thing—Nothing—being the Most Holy Ancient from Whom the Light flows forth.

Yet although every light emanates from this Source, such lights are not in that state of clear shining which would enable man to grasp the nature of the Infinite or the Supreme Will.

The Tree of Life was designed as a ladder of Truth, to help man attain to some understanding of the most Infinite, and the inter-relationship with His Creation. Whether it seems complex or over-simplified, it provides a wonderful approach to attempting this understanding.

The *Keystone of the Tarot with Meditations* is designed to present the essence of Tarot and the Ten Spheres on the Tree of Life, which comprise the first Ten Paths, in the most concise, yet inclusive, manner possible to accompany the twenty-two Keys or Tarot pictures, and explain how to color them. These twenty-two pictures are the Paths numbered eleven through thirty-two, and each picture is a complete lesson in visual form.

"In Thirty-Two wonderful Paths of Wisdom did Jah decree and create His universe, by means of three kinds of characters: Numbers, Letters and Words. To the Ten Spheres of Emanation He assigned Numbers, and these represent the Macrocosm. To the channels between these Spheres, He assigned the 22 Letters, which refer to the relationship between Macrocosm and Microcosm."

The word "Intelligence" used for each Path literally denotes insight or awareness, rather than intellect. The quotations are adapted from the most ancient *Book of Formation*. Paths one through ten refer to the ten Spheres on the Tree of Life; Paths eleven through thirty-two refer to the twenty-two Major Arcana Tarot Keys.

Thirty-Two Paths of Wisdom

32 Paths of Wisdom On the Tree of Life

Path		Color	Symbol	Sphere
1	Crown	white	◎	1
2	Wisdom	gray	✦	2
3	Understanding	blue-violet	♄	3
4	Mercy	blue	♃	4
5	Severity	red	♂	5
6	Beauty	yellow	☉	6
7	Victory	green	♀	7
8	Splendor	orange	☿	8
9	Foundation	purple	☽	9
10	Kingdom (Four Elements)	earth colors	⊗	10

		Color	Key	Hebrew Letter	Letter
11	Fool	yellow	0	א	A
12	Magician	yellow	1	ב	B
13	High Priestess	blue	2	ג	G
14	Empress	green	3	ד	D
15	Emperor	red	4	ה	E
16	Teacher	red-orange	5	ו	V
17	Lovers	orange	6	ז	Z
18	Chariot	orange-yellow	7	ח	Ch
19	Strength	yellow	8	ט	T
20	Hermit	yellow-green	9	י	Y
21	Wheel of Fortune	violet	10	כ	K
22	Justice	green	11	ל	L
23	Suspended Man	blue	12	מ	M
24	Transition	blue-green	13	נ	N
25	Temperance	blue	14	ס	S
26	Deceiver	blue-violet	15	ע	O
27	Tower	red	16	פ	P
28	Star	violet	17	צ	Ts
29	Moon	violet-red	18	ק	Q
30	Sun	orange	19	ר	R
31	Judgement	red	20	ש	Sh
32	World	blue-violet	21	ת	Th

The Ten Spheres of Emanation on the Tree of Life

PATH ONE: The Supreme Crown (in Hebrew, *Kether*) is called "The Admirable, or Wonderful Intelligence. It is the Light of the beginning which is without a beginning—the First Splendor, and the Primordial Intelligence. No created being can attain to its essential Reality."

It is the first Emanation out of the Absolute, the beginning of "Whirlings," or the first movement forth from the Unmanifest toward manifestation. If you are coloring the Tree, this Sphere is usually shown as white.

PATH TWO: Wisdom *(Chokmah)*. "The Illuminating Intelligence, called the Crown of Creation and the Splendor of Supreme Unity, to which it is most in proximity. It is exalted above every head, and is distinguished as the Second Glory."

This Sphere is called the seat of the Father, from which emanates the Life-Force which activates all other parts of the Tree. It is the male aspect of the Creative Principle, and is also known as the Sphere of the Zodiac. The color is gray, a color symbolizing both wisdom and the union of opposites. Jah.

PATH THREE: Understanding *(Binah)* is called "the Sanctifying Intelligence, and is the foundation of Primordial Wisdom, termed the Creation of Faith. Its roots are Amen. It is the Mother of Faith, which emanates therefrom."

This Sphere represents the feminine Creative Principle, wherein the One becomes the many. The Elohim are associated herewith, the Divine soul, and the Great Sea. It is colored indigo, to symbolize form-building qualities.

PATH FOUR: Mercy *(Chesed)* is of Jupiterian nature, and colored blue. It is called "the Measuring, Arresting, or Receiving Intelligence, because it rises like a boundary to receive the emanations of the higher intelligences which are sent down to it, and from whence is the origin of all beneficent power."

This is the Sphere of memory, both Cosmic and personal. It represents not only beneficence of the Great Ones, but Power. As memory, it is the great Akasha, and that consciousness which remembers its Divine Source.

PATH FIVE: Severity *(Geburah)*, colored red, nature of Mars. "The Fifth Path is called the Radical intelligence, because it is more akin than any other to the Supreme Unity, and it is within the substance of Understanding which itself emanates from within the enclosure of the Primordial Wisdom."

This is the realm of Strength, Awe, of Cosmic Justice, and Divine Law. Here is that certainty of justice which may engender fear when one goes against those immutable Laws (not of man). Courage, volition, and will power reside here.

PATH SIX: Beauty *(Tiphareth)*, the Sun-Son. Its color is golden-yellow. This Path is called "the Path of Mediating Influence, because it gathers together the flux of emanations of the Archetypal influence, and communicates this affluence to those blessed men who are united with it."

Beauty represents perfect balance and Equilibrium; the harmony of the Mediating Influence, which gathers all that comes from the Highest Source, and distributes it to those below. The Child forms the third point of a triangle with Wisdom and Understanding, hence the Unity which partakes of both. This is the radical center between Archetypal worlds above, and human and material below.

PATH SEVEN: Victory *(Netzach)* "is called the Occult or Hidden Intelligence, because it pours out a brilliant splendor on all intellectual virtues which are beheld with the eyes of the spirit and by the ecstasy of faith."

Desire is the nature of this Sphere, and it is through right desire that all impulse to accomplish anything arises. It is through victory over the animal within that one is admitted into the fellowship of higher beings, and the realm of higher Wisdom. This Sphere is colored green, the color of Venus.

PATH EIGHT: Splendor *(Hod)*, is colored orange, and relates to Intellect, the balancing factor with desire. Its planet is Mercury. This Path is called "the Perfect and Absolute Intelligence. The preparation of principles emanates therefrom. The roots to which it adheres are in the depths of the Sphere Magnificence from the very substance of which it emanates." This Sphere relates to the first stages of illumination.

PATH NINE: Foundation *(Yesod)* is the "Path of the Purified Intelligence. It purifies the numerations, prevents and stays the fracture of their images, for it establishes their unity, to preserve them from destruction and division by their unity with itself."

This is the plane just above the physical, the realm of the Vital Soul, and the etheric, psychic, or astral realm. It is the plane of contact with higher orders of knowing, through automatic consciousness. Guidance and direction do not come from this plane, but through it, from higher levels. Do not accept anything from the misguided entities of the plane itself. Test them, as John said, in the Light. When asked to stand in the Light, are they still there? This Sphere is colored purple, and is the plane of the Moon.

PATH TEN: Kingdom *(Malkuth)* "is called the Resplendent Intelligence, because it is exalted above every head and has its seat in Understanding. It illuminates the fire of all lights and causes a supply of influence to emanate from the Prince of Countenances."

The Tenth Sphere is the final stage of Creation, the material or physical plane, as the Ninth represented the Formative plane, the Sixth the Creative World, and the First the Archetypal World of pure Idea. Malkuth, Kingdom, is made up of the four elements which emanated from the Ether of outer space. It depicts the perfected manifestation of cosmic forces on the physical plane. The four segments of the circle are colored thus: Air, at top, citron (green plus orange); Fire, at left, russet (orange plus violet); Water, at right, olive (violet plus green); and Earth, at bottom, black.

Coloring The Ten Spheres on the Tree of Life

PATH ONE   Crown *(Kether)*: White

PATH TWO   Wisdom *(Chokmah)*: Gray

PATH THREE   Understanding (Binah): Indigo

PATH FOUR   Mercy *(Chesed)*: Blue

PATH FIVE   Severity *(Geburah)*: Red

PATH SIX   Beauty *(Tiphareth)*: Golden-yellow

PATH SEVEN   Victory *(Netzach)*: Green

PATH EIGHT   Splendor *(Hod)*: Orange

PATH NINE   Foundation *(Yesod)*: Purple

PATH TEN   Kingdom *(Malkuth)*
- Air, at top: Citron (green plus orange)
- Fire, at left: Russet (orange plus violet)
- Water, at right: Olive (violet plus green)
- Earth, at bottom: Black

Paths eleven through thirty-two refer to the twenty-two Major Arcana Tarot Keys, and are colored as noted in the coloring instructions for each Key.

"In Thirty-Two wonderful Paths of Wisdom did Jah decree and create His universe, by means of three kinds of characters: Numbers, Letters and Words. To the Ten spheres of Emanation, He assigned Numbers, and these refer to the Macrocosm. To the channels between these Spheres, He assigned twenty-two Letters, which refer to the relationship between Macrocosm and Microcosm."

Coloring the Ten Spheres on the Tree of Life

Keystone of the Tarot with Meditations

Angshu Purkait/Unsplash

The 78 Cards in the Tarot Deck

In ordinary playing cards, the numbers one to ten are said to correlate with those of the Ten Paths, while the four suits of clubs, hearts, spades, and diamonds relate to the four elements of Fire, Water, Air and Earth—respectively. When we deal with the Tarot or older European decks of playing cards, the clubs become Wands; the hearts, Cups; the spades, Swords; and the diamonds—hardest substance of natural manifestation—become Coins.

There are 78 cards in a full set of the Tarot, most of them akin to the regular playing cards, with four Kings and Queens; but instead of Jacks, there are both four Knights and four Pages. These cards are called the Minor Arcana, and again relate to the four elements in a different way. The word "arcane" refers to the secrets of nature, or to mysteries beyond ordinary human experience.

But added to the set are 22 cards which seem not directly related to any of the others. These are the trumps, or Major Arcana, twenty-two pictures correlated with the letters of the Hebrew alphabet. On these is based the study of Tarot, the twenty-two Paths summed up in a word similar to "Tao," which means the Way.

It is believed that certain Priests and Teachers of ancient Orders, entrusted with the preservation of their teachings through unpredictable times, used the simple method of hiding the sacred Mysteries in plain sight by slipping them among a set of picture cards used for gaming. Only the initiate, who would easily recognize the symbols, could guess their secret—the "apparent folly of the very wise." The Fool himself gives this away.

There is also a possibility the whole set of seventy-eight was designed for spiritual teaching, and merely fell to the lot of a gaming device. Their actual origin is lost in ancient times, though many nations claim them, in particular the Near-Eastern countries.

By depicting these Truths in pictures, the Initiate was enabled to surmount language barriers, for every eye can see the symbols alike. These symbols themselves are common to all Wisdom teachings, and certain evidences are found in the pictures which tie them in with many philosophies.

Coloring the Major Arcana Tarot Keys

When coloring the pictures, take them in numeric order and follow instructions carefully. While working with them in orderly fashion, their meanings begin to unfold in sequence within your own subconscious, striking chords of recollection in the soul.

These colors are not chosen for artistic values, but for interior meanings—so never try to change or "improve upon" them. For example, white is for purity, blue for memory, red for action, etc., plus other meanings, as given with the individual pictures.

Flesh color for light skin is a very diluted orange, almost all water. Flesh color for darker skin is a very diluted brown. Try it on something else before placing it on the picture, and keep a facial tissue handy for blotting if needed. Flesh color is used on all skin areas, except in Keys 6 and 20 where noted.

When coloring backgrounds and sky, dilute quite thin to avoid "heavy" appearance, and work fast on these areas to prevent streaking. It seems impossible with water colors and acrylics to avoid some streaks.

Blonde hair color is achieved by adding a little brown to yellow. Gold and silver should be water color, not enamel or oil-based paint. Eagle Prismacolor pencils are also good for this and easy to apply, available in gold, silver and copper. If you cannot obtain either, use yellow for gold, and white for silver.

Acrylics, or water (poster) colors usually work best for the pictures, acrylics being a little more durable. Some like to use felt-tip pens, but with these it is hard to achieve a delicate touch. One may use them for parts of a picture along with water colors.

On thin paper use crayons or coloring pencils to avoid soaking or wrinkling the paper, but choose them carefully for your purpose. Coloring pencils may require going over a second time in the opposite direction to obtain sufficient depth.

A small error may be corrected with a touch of white-out, when color is dry. Where water color was used (not acrylics) some color may be removed by soaking picture face down overnight in water. Always practice with the colors on something dispensable first, rather than to risk a picture, especially the first ones. Work slowly when you can relax and enjoy it, to gain more understanding and a better picture.

The better or more expensive brands of acrylics usually come in "art" name-colors, which prove a little difficult for this purpose, being off-shade. Try to obtain true or primary colors in RED, YELLOW, BLUE, GREEN, VIOLET, BROWN, BLACK and WHITE, plus GOLD and SILVER water colors or Eagle pencils. These complete the needs. Orange is easily mixed by blending red and yellow, and is not needed in any amount. Get other shades only if you can afford them; for example, gray is nice to have, and a second shade of blue, and of green.

To keep expenses down still further, omit green and violet from your list of purchases, and mix them yourself: green can be obtained from blue-plus-yellow; and violet from red-plus-blue. Any further reduction is more in the way of experimentation, but it is possible to make your own brown by mixing red, yellow, and blue, and finding the right proportion. These same three primary colors can be used to make gray by adding a little more blue. For dark gray add a touch of black. In this case, your list is reduced to rock-bottom essentials of red, yellow, blue, black, and white.

Have at least two or three soft, good-quality water color brushes, such as sable or camel's hair. One of them very fine, one medium, and one larger for backgrounds.

When using acrylics, if desired, Hyslo Acrylic Retarder keeps color from drying too fast, and polymer medium adds a little luster, but neither is important. Gel medium is useless for these pictures. Use plastic, glass or porcelain to mix colors in, and have plenty of water for clean brushes. Keep them moist, for acrylics dry fast. To lighten shades do not add white, which makes colors opaque; thin rather with more water, or purchase a lighter shade.

Coloring is a valuable part of the study, as it enables you to build the spiritual meaning into your consciousness. If you also meditate five minutes daily on the Key you are studying, this more fully unfolds its meaning. To gaze longer than that at a picture is not useful, but one may meditate with eyes closed for another ten minutes or so.

May you experience the joy of discovering Truth of yourself, for the real Treasure is hidden within.

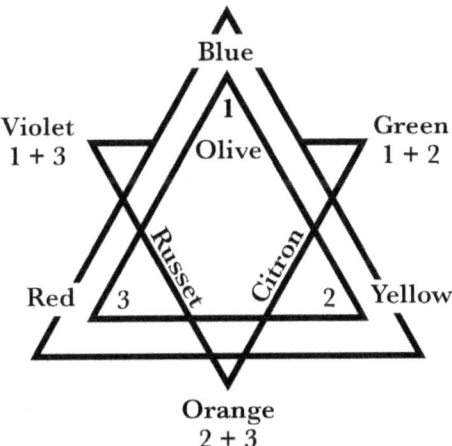

The above chart shows how colors are mixed. For example, primary colors red and blue mixed together make the secondary color, violet; while secondary colors, violet and green together, make the tertiary color, olive.

COLOR SYMBOLOGY IN A NUTSHELL

Red: Usually indicates action, courage, strength, and physical energy. The fire element. Nature of the planet Mars.

Orange: Red plus yellow; positive energy and vitality; authority; primarily solar, with some Mercury influence.

Yellow: Mental equilibrium, intellect, element of Air, Mercury, sometimes solar energy.

Green: Blue plus yellow; growth, increase, emotion, desire, the Harmony of Nature. Venus.

Blue: Water; memory, receptivity, and reflection. Moon. Jupiter.

Blue-violet or Indigo: The First Matter; the akasha. Saturn.

Violet: Spiritual power; truth. This is the highest visible color vibration. Beyond that is ultra violet. Jupiter. Neptune.

Silver: The Lunar currents. Moon.

Gold: The Solar forces.

White: Purity, and the Primal Light. Pure Spirit.

Black: Primal Matter: the occult or unknown; the element.

Brown: Of earthly nature.

Gray: Wisdom; the union of opposites.

Coloring the Major Arcana Tarot Keys

Clear bright colors have more positive meaning.

Primary colors are red, yellow and blue.

Secondary colors, orange, green, and violet, are produced by combining two primary colors.

Tertiary colors, citron, olive, and russet, are produced by combining two secondary colors.

The Twenty-Two Keys

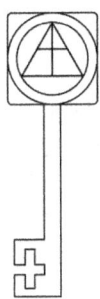

The Fool   Aleph
0

Number Zero: This key relates to the Cosmic Egg, or undeveloped Potential of the All.

Path of Wisdom 11, the Fiery or Scintillating Intelligence, wherewith one comes face to face with the Cause of Causes.

Letter A, in Hebrew "Aleph," which means "ox," is a symbol for natural Creative Energy and motive Power. It is one of the three Mother Letters, the Element Air in its original state.

Numerical value of the letter Aleph is 1, as the first letter of the Hebrew alphabet.

Identity: Superconsciousness, or Spirit in search of experience. Pure Conscious Energy; Breath; Primal Will; the First Manifestation of Life Power, forever young.

Astrologically: The planet Uranus, named from root word meaning "heaven." Ruler of Aquarius, of electricity, space, of this Age, and unfoldment of the God-given powers of Man.

SYMBOLOGY OF THE COLORS AND ELEMENTS

Background: Yellow color indicates radiant energy of Air, used in breathing.

White Sun: Universal Radiant Energy, Kether, the Crown. The Spiritual Sun.

Wand: Symbol of Will and measurement. Black for occult powers.

Wallet: Summed-up experience. Essence of former existence. Memory. Soul. Subconscious.

Rose: White shows unfoldment of purified desire nature; suggests where he came from.

Green wreath: On head, binding of sunlight and Life-Power in Nature.

White inner gown: Purity and perfect Wisdom.

Black outer robe: Ignorance and dense matter. Red lining: passion and force.

IHVH: The Divine Name, or Yahweh, in Hebrew, on gown at throat. Also called the Tetragrammaton, which means "four-lettered," and is associated with the Hebrew word "to be."

Eight-pointed Star at shoulder: Solar, or electric, current of energy.

Lunar crescent at shoulder: Magnetic current. Solar (electric) and lunar (magnetic) together: two modes of the Life-Force.

Wheels on robe: Solar orbs. Eight spokes, whirling orbs of Creation. One wheel contains a triple flame, correlating One Force with Fire and Light. One contains the Hebrew letter Shin, the Mother Letter for Fire in its original state, and also a symbol of the Holy Spirit.

Belt: He is girded with temporary limitation of Time, and the Zodiac.

Dog: Intellect, friendly companion, far less than true Self.

The Abyss: Refers to the subconscious mind, to Nature, and to activity. The valley of experience.

The Twenty-Two Keys—The Fool: Key 0

His face is turned northwestward, the direction of new enterprises, and his consciousness never drops.

The Goal to which he attains is higher than his present position, as shown by his gaze, but he must first traverse the valley of experience.

"Before Abraham was, I AM." (John 8:58)

"If any one among you thinks that he is wise in this age, let him become a fool that he may become wise." (1 Corinthians 3:18)

COLORING INSTRUCTIONS

While coloring this first Key, test each color on something else before using on your picture.

White:	The area inside the egg-shaped radiance may be colored same as background, or preferably left white. Sun, inner garment, dog, rose, mountain peaks, eye on flap of pouch.
Yellow:	Background; circles on garment (except flame in top circle); shoes.
Green:	Leaves surrounding circles on outer garment and other tendril-like figures, leaves on rose; wreath around head.
Violet:	Mountains. (Use somewhat diluted solution since they are distant mountains. The peaks are snow-capped, so do not paint where snow is to be.)
Brown:	Eagle on wallet, precipice in foreground upon which the Fool stands.
Flesh:	Hands and face.

Blond:	Hair; eagle's beak and claws.
Citron:	Hose (this is a mixture of orange and green, and is the only place it is used except on the 10th Sphere of the Tree of Life).
Gold:	Star on shoulder. Knob of staff. Belt.
Silver:	Moon on shoulder.
Red:	Feather, lining of outer garment, spokes of wheels, flame in top circle, wallet (except for eagle and eye).
Black:	Staff, except knob and white strip lengthwise.

The color of Path 11 on the Tree of Life is yellow.

MEDITATION

Aleph am I, the A of AUM, the Source,
The Primal Vital Force of all that is.
Life Breath, and Spirit Fire, before beginnings,
Bound not, held not by time nor form.

When I don the robe of matter to descend,
These feet, shod with the human intellect,
Store and distill all memories of experience,
To their bare essence in the pouch of soul.

My consciousness descendeth not,
But riseth ever on to further heights.

The Magician   Beth

1   

Number One: The number 1 is a single upright figure, being the first extension from a point. It is a vertical line, connecting Height and Depth on the Cube of Space.

Path of Wisdom 12: This is known as the Intelligence of Transparency or of Light, and "the source of vision in those who behold apparitions."

Letter B, in Hebrew "Beth," which means "house," or "abode," and relates to the thinking apparatus and personality wherein we dwell, and temple of the living God.

Numerical value of the letter Beth is 2, as the second letter of the Hebrew alphabet.

Identity: Intellect or self-conscious mind. You as actor or doer of anything.

Function: Attention, beginning, initiative, concentration. Your mind is your magician, and kindler of the fire.

Astrologically: The planet Mercury, messenger of the gods, and planet of the Intellect. It is identified with Hermes and Thoth. As Thoth, he works out the creation as decreed by the Sun god, Ra.

SYMBOLOGY OF THE COLORS AND ELEMENTS

Background is shown yellow, signifying the element Air, and mental enlightenment.

Roses are red, the color of action and energy. They also signify the desire nature.

Outer garment is red, for he needs energy to act and begin the work.

Inner garment is white, showing the underlying purity needed for this work.

His headband is also white, indicating the light and purity which is used to bind back the dense locks of ignorance and inertia, its wings referring to the evolutive motion of Air, and to Mercury as winged messenger of thought.

The white wand uplifted symbolizes the sublimated reproductive forces, and allowing his will to be used as a hollow channel for the Will of God.

Figure 8 over his head is a symbol of infinity, of involution and evolution.

The serpent girdle, or belt, is a symbol of Eternity, and of regenerative Force. He accepts Eternity as the framework within which he acts.

The man's figure represents your house of personality as a center through which the Spirit of your own true Self expresses itself. You are a channel through which universal Creative Force is directed to planes below the level of human consciousness, and through which the transmuting and transforming power of attention takes place. Things are as we see them.

The bench, or table, is the drawing board of an artist or an engineer, his Trestleboard. The tools of his craft placed thereon depict the four elements or Principles in nature—Fire, Water, Air, and Earth. These also depict the four suits of playing cards

The Magician was also known in ancient times as the Alchemist, or Juggler.

The tools are: Fire—the white wand signifying Will; Water—the silver chalice symbolizing imagination and knowing; Air the steel sword of daring and formation; Earth—the silent coin of dense materialization.

The garden below is the subconscious field cultivated by his attention.

Its flowers are the red roses, which are also above, of human love and desire for action; they are five-petalled. The six-petalled lilies depict pure thought, and divine love. Their green leaves show growth.

Part of the lesson of Key 1 is that of hewing-out for yourself a "place," whether in space or time, in which to perform any particular work. It needn't be a physically established place, but everything you give attention to begins to manifest some outer aspect of "dwelling" with you. Keeping all tools neatly in order saves time and makes you more skillful in their use.

> *The Bible says: "Except the Lord build the House, he labors in vain who builds it." (Psalm 127:1)*

> *"In essence God is one, and all forms are naught but transmutations and variations of a single Essence."*

COLORING INSTRUCTIONS

Yellow: Background, spear head, and lily stamens.

Green: Foliage.

Blue-green: Serpent belt.

Brown: Work bench.

White: Inner garment, head band, spear shaft, wand, lilies.

Gold: Sword handle, circle at the end of spear shaft, coin on table.

Silver: Cup. Pentagram traced on coin; circle on head band.

Steel: Sword blade (a little blue mixed with gray).

Red: Outer garment and roses.

The color of Path 12 on the Tree of Life is yellow.

MEDITATION

As Beth I am thy House of thought and personality,
The Dwelling Place of Divine Life-Breath,
Receiver and transmitter of the Will-to-Good,
One only, changeless, indivisible am I.

On my drawing bench the tools are laid,
The mixing bowl of elements,
That through attention manifold expressions
May flow unending from Above.

O Lord, I love the habitation of Thy house,
The place where Thy Glory dwells.

HIGH PRIESTESS   GIMEL

2

Number Two: 2 carries the idea of duality, reflection, response, and repetition.

Path of Wisdom 13: This Path is called the Uniting Intelligence—"the Essence of Glory, and perfection of the Truths of Spiritual Unities."

Letter G, in Hebrew "Gimel," means "camel." This suggests a link between places, commerce and communication.

Numerical value of the letter Gimel is 3, as the third letter of the Hebrew alphabet.

Identity: She represents the Soul and the subconscious mind, dwelling within the temple of God. Her blue background denotes unmanifest Sound.

Astrologically: She represents the Moon. She is also the Third Veil of Light, AUR, as shown by the white undergown representing Light.

SYMBOLOGY OF THE COLORS AND ELEMENTS

The blue of her robe represents primary root-substance or cosmic Mind-Stuff, of which the Universe is made up.

The element Water is indicated as symbolic of all these attributes, this Water on the Key being the source of all rivers and pools in all Keys.

She represents the Moon goddess, Diana; the Mother Isis and other goddesses.

Her crown is of silver, metal of the moon—the crown of Isis with waxing and waning crescents, the full moon between. She reflects and duplicates as the moon reflects sunlight. The stars on her gown depict sunlight reflected on water.

The diamond on the crown, over the pineal gland, is used here to symbolize the Moon Center, and suggests the spiritual treasure and riches of the light of wisdom, which contains all flashing colors in its pure knowing.

The gray veil behind her is the veil before the inner sanctuary and denotes virginal purity and primal substance. The Wise Virgin.

The veil's gray color reflects the Sphere of Wisdom, Chokmah, and the High Priestess is sometimes called the lesser Wisdom as the feminine aspect of all that the Life Power is. The color also refers to the union or the reconciliation of opposites (as black plus white).

The palms (male) and the pomegranates (female) emphasize opposite polarities.

The pillars represent all pairs of opposites, such as Light and Darkness. The Priestess between acts as the equilibrating power between Initiative and Resistance.

The white pillar displays the letter Yod, initial of Jachin, the positive or establishing principle of Thought. Yod means "hand." Atop it is a brazier of Fire. Jachin was the father of Mary.

The black pillar shows the letter Beth, initial of Boaz, which translates as "in a strength." This Strength is rooted in resistance. Beth means "house." Atop the pillar is a basin of water indicating the passive polarity. Boaz was husband of Ruth.

The two great pillars called Boaz and Jachin symbolize the polarity in nature which is the means of productivity. Isis as the "world virgin" sits between them to show the Truth that is found between opposite extremes, or the divine nature of man crucified between contradictory influences. All action is rooted in the opposition of forces, whether physical or spiritual. Between these is the veiled entrance to the Holy Place of God.

Lotus buds near the top of each pillar show the potential in subconsciousness; latent undeveloped powers.

The cubical seat shows the solidness of material creation from which she works. Order and truth. Alchemical "salt," earth, crystallizes into cubes.

Cube and column rest upon a yellow-colored foundation of mental activity.

The spiral-roll of the scroll shows the Life-Power's whirling nature, from the Center outward, while the scroll itself stands for the power of recollection.

Tora means "law." The laws of nature are the Life-Power's perfect memory of orderly sequences.

"Faith is the Substance of all things hoped for." (Hebrews 11:1)

"The One Life only seemeth to divide itself, becoming two; that in the Divine Mirror of Mine own substance innumerable images might show forth." (I Kings 7:15)

COLORING INSTRUCTIONS

Yellow: Left foreground, streaks in flame atop right pillar.

Green: Palms (not centers), on veil behind Priestess.

Blue: Background. Robe. The robe should have white streaks in it where it shimmers down in front and out of the picture, to represent flowing water. Water in bowl on left pillar, same. Leave gown white over her right leg and knee.

Gray: Throne and veil in background. (Veil may be left unpainted.)

White: Inner garment, cross on breast, head veil, right pillar, Hebrew letter on left pillar. Palm centers. Stars on hem of gown. Gown over chest, and her right leg (on your left), diamond on crown.

Silver: Crown, and bowl atop black pillar.

Bronze or Gold: Brazier atop white pillar. (Bronze is copper, plus a little yellow.)

Brown: Scroll (much diluted to look like parchment).

Red: Pomegranates (seeds deeper red), streaks in flame.

The color of Path 13 on the Tree of Life is blue.

MEDITATION

Gimel, I'm called, the Camel and the knowing
Which beareth travelers along life's Way,
And links the destination with the Source.

I am the Stream of Consciousness, unaltered by experience,
Whose Virgin Substance mirrors to Itself God's Will.
My perfect recollection is the Root of Wisdom.

When my One Life seemeth to divide, becoming two,
Ama, my perfect Wisdom, floweth forth
Uniting that which but appears contrary,
Balancing dark of matter with the Spirit's Light.

THE EMPRESS   DALETH
3   ד

Number Three. 3 denotes increase, productivity, growth, and understanding.

Path of Wisdom 14: Operating between Chokmah and Binah, this Path is called the Luminous Intelligence, and the foundation of holiness.

Letter D, in Hebrew "Daleth," (in Greek Delta) means "door," that which permits passage, ingress and egress; in or out.

The numerical value of the letter Daleth is 4, the fourth letter of the Hebrew alphabet.

Identity: The Empress is Mother of Ideas, the generatrix of mental images. She represents the productive aspect of the subconscious and, as the womb, represents the doorway to this world.

Astrologically: She represents the planet Venus, beauty, fruitfulness, and growth.

SYMBOLOGY OF THE COLORS AND ELEMENTS

The gateway of form is the portal through which Life enters the realm of limited creation.

She faces the direction East, the point of sunrise, the dawn of higher consciousness.

Yellow background denotes a condition proceeding from thought.

Cypress trees are sacred to Venus, as are the evergreen myrtle leaves forming the wreath on her head, also tokens of immortality.

Yellow hair shows radiant energy, bound by the green leaves of Cosmic energy working at the subconscious level.

Stars of the crown are six-pointed, to show attainment in using laws of the macrocosm. Twelve of them signify the zodiac, or 12 modes of energy by which she is influenced. Celestial forces.

The scepter shows the globe of this world, or dominion over the physical plane, surmounted by a cross. The Venus symbol, upside down.

Pearls are related to the Moon and to Venus, seven a Venus number, for the original planets and for the seven chakras. They are strung in order at the door of the throat, ruled by Venus.

The copper shield, a metal assigned to Venus, denotes love as her defense, and the desire nature whose negative trend led to the fall. Positively used, this force is the urge-to-good which brings about redemption. It has seven sides to show the number of Venus. The dove represents the Holy Spirit, or Life Force. Here it's seen moving on the shield of love, not in the head. Meaning is found in the heart. Waist and neckline edged in gold—"clothed with the Sun."

The green of her gown is the color of Venus, a combination of Mercury, which is yellow, and Moon, which is blue, to produce Venus' green, "sea-born."

The red triangle is the Greek letter Delta. It also suggests universal energy operating through the Law of the Triangle in the heart area.

Wheat shows the multiplication of original seed. Growth.

The stone bench is an artistic "improvement on nature."

Green is a color of symmetry and balance, occupying the central position in the solar spectrum, midway between hot fiery red and cold electrical violet. Thus it symbolizes peace and harmony, further attributes of Venus, as well as growth and abundance. Green is the color most used in nature for vegetation, which has a healthy effect of purifying the air.

On the Tree of Life, green is the color of the Venus Sphere called Victory, which relates to the desire nature.

"And a great portent appeared in heaven, a woman clothed with the sun, with the moon under her feet, and on her head a crown of twelve stars, she was with child…" (Revelation 12:1)

COLORING INSTRUCTIONS

Yellow: Background, slipper, staff of scepter.

Green: Foliage, grass, wreath (leave sandy space beside the waterfall). Robe (except cuffs, girdle, collar edging and panel). Ball on scepter (not bar and cross.)

Blue: Stream and waterfall; irises of eyes.

Brown: Tree trunks; sandy slope beside waterfall.

Gray: Stone bench.

Gold: Stars, collar edging, girdle, cross and bar on scepter.

Silver: Crescent.

Copper: Shield (except symbol). Mixture of gold, red, and brown obtains copper.

Blonde: Hair, wheat ears.

White: Pearls, panel in dress, cuffs of dress, symbol on shield, highlights in waterfall.

Red: Roses, triangle on breast.

The color of Path 14 on the Tree of Life is green.

MEDITATION

Daleth, my name, means Door,
The Gateway of true Understanding
Through which Eternal Life must enter into form,
Binding Itself in earthly semblance for a while
To gain through wide experience its growth.

They call me Aima, fruitful, radiant
Soul-Mother of all that is to come,
The Son of God within me bides
Waiting to step through Dawn's bright portals
When the luminous threads of My Creative Thought
Have spun a vesture fit for his abode.

The Emperor   Heh
4

Number Four. 4 is the number which symbolizes order, establishment, reason, and manifestation.

Path of Wisdom 15: This Path is called the Constituting Intelligence because "it constitutes Creation in the darkness of the world."

Letter E, in Hebrew "Heh," or silent H, means "window." It is the second and fourth letter of the Tetragrammaton.

The numerical value of the letter Heh is 5, the fifth letter of the Hebrew alphabet.

Function: Sight is the function of this Key, a window admitting Light and permitting observation. Sight also permits supervision, measurement, and accurate classification.

Astrologically: He represents Aries, first sign of the zodiac, and symbol of the outgoing emanation of Primal Will at the beginning of Cosmic manifestation.

SYMBOLOGY OF THE COLORS AND ELEMENTS

The Monarch ruling the Kingdom represents your own true Self, who must take steps to establish the dominion over his own universe, through the two main functions of this Key: Order and Reason.

He is both the Ancient of Days, and the youth of Spring Eternal. His posture suggests the number 4 and the symbol for alchemical Sulphur.

He sits overlooking the stream of consciousness stemming from the High Priestess' robe, which has watered the Empress' garden.

The orange background is a solar color combining red with yellow, reminding us that the Sun is exalted in Aries. It is also a color of pride and vitality.

Red mountains show the nature of a Fire sign. These are igneous rock, formed from the solidification of molten rock material, which are disintegrating and becoming the soil for the cultivated garden. In the same manner must pure Reason be broken down into its elements, and mixed with emotional qualities in order to produce results.

The 12 points on the helmet, of which six are visible, correspond to the Empress' 12 stars. An Aries symbol is on top, and the gold trim is the metal of the Sun.

Steel armor is the metal of Mars, which rules Aries, a warrior planet.

The violet of his garb is symbolic of royalty, and hints at the idea of Truth as his defense, for violet is a color associated with Aquarius and Truth.

The cubical seat is suggestive of the number 4, and is a symbol of form. It is also of stone, the "ehben" which hints at the mysterious Stone of the Philosopher, in the union of Father (eh) and Son (ben).

The red eagle represents swift, creative energy, the initiative of all being, and the red tincture of the alchemist.

His scepter is a modified Venus symbol, the Egyptian Ankh, a sign of Life.

The globe shows dominion over earthly affairs and all below his level.

Tetragrammaton means "four lettered." JHVH, or Yahweh, commonly but incorrectly called Jehovah, was the Divine Name by which the Creator was known to the Hebrews. Its true pronunciation has been forgotten because only the high priest was ever allowed to speak it. It is associated with the Hebrew verb "to be," and in its entirety is translated as "that which was, that which is, and that which shall be."

"The city lies foursquare, its length the same as its breadth; and he measured the city with his rod..."
(New Jerusalem Bible, Revelation 21:16)

"...the glory of God is its light, and its lamp is the Lamb."
(Revelation 23:23)

COLORING INSTRUCTIONS

Yellow: Tau cross and circle in his right hand.

Green: Foreground.

Blue: Stream.

Gray: Stone cube.

Violet: Belt and outer garments, except borders.

White: Edging of cloak and hem of tunic; undersleeve; beard and hair; ram; border of inverted T in globe; shield on ground (except eagle).

Gold: Inverted T and cross on globe; framework and points on helmet.

Brown: Sandy slopes between grassy area in foreground and edge of stream.

Orange: Upper background.

Steel: Leg armor and breastplate.

Red: Mountains; globe in left hand (not inverted T or cross); helmet (except borders and points); eagle.

The color of Path 15 on the Tree of Life is red.

MEDITATION

Heh is a window, open to admit clear light
To those who watch with inner eyes to see.
Its curtains only closed to the profane
Not yet prepared to witness greater Truth.

He reigns with reason to establish order,
Versed in the power of the Creative Word
Whose Fire lays down the framework of the worlds.

He rules as father, armed with Truth
and measuring with Love,
Established in the four-square name Yod Heh Vav Heh,
He watches and commands, and then lifts up His Son.

The Teacher

5

Vav

Number Five: 5 is the middle number between 1 and 9; thus it symbolizes a mediator, and man as between God and nature: The Law.

Path of Wisdom 16: This Path is termed the triumphant and Eternal Intelligence, "The delight of glory, and the garden of pleasure prepared for the just."

Letter V, in Hebrew "Vav," is the third letter of the Tetragrammaton. In English it is U, V, or W. Vav means "nail" or "hook," sometimes also used as the conjunction "and" to join things together.

The numerical value of the letter Vav is 6, the sixth letter in the Hebrew alphabet.

Identity: He is both the Initiate, or Master, over the mystery of Life, and the Teacher within oneself; the One Self, and the Inner Voice. The two fingers raised in blessing show that all is not at once outwardly revealed; a part is shown, some must be sought. As mediator it is his job to form a link between microcosm and macrocosm.

Function: Hearing is the function of this Key, and the Intuition which must follow reason and go beyond. "He that hath an ear, let him hear."

Astrologically: He represents the sign Taurus, the fixed Earth sign. Two horned symbols of this sign adorn the upper corners of the throne.

SYMBOLOGY OF THE COLORS AND ELEMENTS

The gray background suggests emanation from Chokmah, Sephirah of Paternal Wisdom, and gray shows the union of black and white, Spirit and matter—known and unknown, all opposites reconciled.

The crown of authority is of golden yellow color, like solar energy. Its four folds signify: at top the idea; in the second row the nature of the Life-Power; third row, the modes of manifestation; last row, the Spirits of God. He is intended to depict no specific religion, but a Universal Teacher.

The crossbars of the golden staff indicate the same four levels, the archetypal being shown by the knob on top. It also represents the dominion of the Creative Life Power over the three planes of nature, and its penetration through all of the planes.

The silver moon at the throat points out the exaltation of the Moon in Taurus, its place of highest expression. The thyroid area relates to interior hearing and intuition.

His robe and platform are the red-orange color assigned to Taurus on the color wheel, which begins with red at Aries, and progresses through the 12 signs.

The blue-green border is of the opposite and complementary color and sign, and refers to the Kundalini.

His blue garment represents the Akashic substance and memory.

The white undergarment shows enlightenment and underlying purity as its requirement.

The yokes on the backs of the student-priests refer to a primitive form of the letter Vav, as a fastening or link (yoga or "union")—the uniting of personal consciousness to universal energy. They are shaped just like an ancient form of the letter Vav.

Their color is yellow, the symbol of mental energy.

The Student at left wears a green robe, to represent the growth aspect of the desire nature, while red roses denote the activity thereof.

The red robe on the Student at right shows the fiery aspect of Spirit as a background for lilies of pure thought and devotional nature.

The Students are being directed by the One Self, the Teacher within, who holds up two fingers in a gesture of benediction.

Crosses on the teacher's hand and on his shoes denote union of positive and negative forces, with the resultant order.

The dais is four-square with a diamond design to represent the hardness of earth in a state of highest refinement, the "fixed" earth of Taurus.

Crosses on the carpet are Venus symbols folded over to look like Earth symbols.

The crossed keys of St. Peter show the union of solar and lunar forces, as keys to unlock the inner doors to higher consciousness, and the inner doctrine which acts as a key to the sacred writings of the scriptures.

"For the people shall dwell in Zion at Jerusalem; thou shalt weep no more; he will be very gracious unto thee at the voice of thy cry; when he shall hear it, he will answer thee." (Isaiah 30: 19)

And, read Ecclesiastes 12.

COLORING INSTRUCTIONS

Yellow: Turban or Crown, except top. Flap hanging over one ear, except inside fold. Staff in left hand, and the Y's on the students' garments.

Green: Robe of monk in left foreground (except collar and cuff, flowers, and Y). Foliage on garment at right.

Violet: Inside fold of hanging scarf.

Gray: Background (light), pillars and throne (darker).

Gold: Key with handle at left; small rounded top of turban. Stars in handles.

Silver: Crescent, and key with handle at right, except stars.

Blue: Gown covering knees.

Blue-green: Cuffs of robe, and border extending down the front and around neck.

Brown: Hair of students.

White: Undergarment at throat, sleeves and hem. Shoes, collar, and cuffs of monks. Lilies on student's robe. Tops of their heads.

Red-orange: Robe and carpeting.

Red: Roses on garment at left. Robe of monk at right.

The color of Path 16 on the Tree of Life is red-orange.

MEDITATION

*Vav is the Nail which joins man to God
And links Creation's many parts together.*

*He is the Teacher who instructs all thy paths
By day and night, while sleeping or awake,
When ears are turned away from worldly din
And listen for the secret Voice within
To hear its silent Counseling.*

*With keys of gold and silver, forged by Sun and Moon,
God openeth the treasure of sacred Mysteries
For those who seek His Wisdom faithfully.*

THE LOVERS   ZAIN
6

Number Six: 6 brings out the idea of equilibrium, beauty and reciprocity.

Path of Wisdom 17: This Path on the Tree of Life is called the Intelligence of Sensation, or the Disposing Intelligence. "It disposes the compassionate to perseverance, and clothes them with the Holy Life Breath."

Letter Z: In Hebrew, "Zain" means "sword." Here the One Life seems to divide itself, cutting asunder to "pose apart" temporarily for growth.

The numerical value of the letter Zain is 7, the 7th letter in the Hebrew alphabet.

Identity: This Key represents the power of choice, correct discrimination—or discernment—and the sense of smell. Adam and Eve before the fall.

Astrologically: This Key represents Gemini, the heavenly Twins, a mental air sign.

SYMBOLOGY OF THE COLORS AND ELEMENTS

The angel represents Superconsciousness, or the Mind of God, shedding influence upon both consciousness (the man) and subconsciousness (the woman). These two aspects of human personality are different, but equal.

Raphael is the archangel's name, and it means "God as Healer." He is the archangel of Mercury and Air. He breathes the message that true healing is the attainment of inner and outer wholeness.

Lovers, not opponents, suggest right adjustment, a symbol of mental health. Love is the amalgamating force which brings things to unity.

Behind the angel is the golden force of the Sun, the physical source of Life and energy on earth, and the actual body of the invisible Spiritual Sun.

The angel's yellow skin refers to the element Air and Gemini.

The flames of his hair are a blend of red, for reason; green for imagination; and yellow for light. The tiara of golden feathers at front acts as a focus of attention for the healing powers.

The violet robe indicates Truth, royalty, and dominion. Red wings show right action, the evolutive power of air.

A cloud hides part of the greater powers until man has fully developed, and provides the angel's resting place.

The tree behind the woman shows the Knowledge of Good and Evil with the fruits of the five senses which tempt the subconscious mind through remembered or suggested sensation.

The serpent is of a color symbolizing the desire nature. It also depicts the serpent force of the Kundalini, which, lifted up, is a source of power. When it led the instincts astray through subtle delusion, it was brought low. Green refers to the unripe aspect of that force.

Behind the man is the Tree of Life, with its twelve manner of fruits for the twelve signs of the zodiac, as mentioned in Revelation 22:2, "The leaves of the Tree serve for healing of the nations."

Before them lies the field (the green of imagination) which they must till until the day of the Return to the Father as enlightened beings.

The Bible is a story of the circuit of man from the time he left the Tree until he returns to it, from Genesis to Revelation.

ARCHANGEL OF AIR

O Raphael, speaker of Messages,
Who carriest God's breath to man,
Propelled by His merest Thought—
Who beareth Sound upon thy wings
And drive all scents before thee.
Fragrance heralds thy passing-by,
Yet who sees either wind or you?

Your action swift and bright,
Feathers of motion, fingers of thought
Tousle the sunkist tree tops playfully,
To precious oxygen for health of man.
Your watchful attention cleans the atmosphere
And charges it with God.

COLORING INSTRUCTIONS

Yellow: Five fruits on the tree at left are yellow with red blush. Flames on the other Tree are yellow with red at the base. The angel's flesh is very diluted yellow. The angel's hair is yellow, red, and green flames.

Blue: Background (except above angel's head).

Green: Foreground and foliage, serpent around tree, portion of angel's hair.

Violet: Angel's garment; mountain is more diluted.

Gold: Sun and background above angel. Feather tiara of angel, more shiny in upper half.

White: Clouds.

Blonde: Woman's hair.

Brown: Left tree trunk.

Red: Angel's wings. Parts of angel's hair and fruits.

Black: Man's hair.

The color of Path 17 on the Tree of Life is orange.

MEDITATION

Zain is the fiery Sword, the gift of choice
Set to discern between the false and true.
His swift, bright action flashes forth
To sever chaff from grain, to prune unwanted growth.

The Sword of sharp decision, used by parent birds
To separate hatchlings from their cozy nest
That they may find their own wings to fly free,
Is the same that drives mankind up heaven's Stair.

Adam and Eve, their two hands move apart
For Breath of healing Air to flow between
Brought by the airy Spirit Raphael
Who comes from God with love, the only Power
That bridges every gap and reunites all one.

The Chariot   Cheth

7

Number Seven: 7 is a number of poise, mastery, and victory. The Sabbath—a pause for worship, rest, and recreation.

Path of Wisdom 18: This Path on the Tree of Life is called the Intelligence of the House of Influence. "From the blue interior walls of its perfections were drawn the arcana and concealed meanings reposing in the shadow thereof."

Letter Ch: In Hebrew, "Cheth" means a "fenced field" or "enclosure." One protects with a fence that which he wishes to develop.

The numerical value of the letter Cheth is 8, the 8th letter in the Hebrew alphabet.

Identity: The Chariot represents man's outer vehicle, within which stands the King triumphant, the Self, which through the perfect Will of God, is Master over all. The field is the universe.

Function: Speech is one of the functions of this Key, in the sense of enclosing a thought with words in order to define it, or build a fence around it.

Astrologically: This Key represents the sign of Cancer, a water sign ruled by the Moon. It refers to the protection of the mother-aspect.

SYMBOLOGY OF THE COLORS AND ELEMENTS

The One Self guides his vehicle using invisible reins of mind to control the senses.

The yellow background indicates the thought which precedes Speech. The stream flowing past is the consciousness which permits growth of his field of influence, and again refers to the Moon.

The starry canopy shows celestial forces which are, in fact, all around us, descending into physical levels through the activity of the four elements, as the cause of physical manifestation.

The four pillars support this, each ringed with the One Spirit.

The Chariot of stone "ehben," (Father-Son), acts as a movable "fence" for the Ego.

The crown has three golden pentagrams, mental dominion over natural forces.

Lunar crescents on the shoulders show phases of the Moon, ruler of Cancer and of the female organs.

His breastplate is green-yellow to represent brass, the Venus metal, and provides the protective power of creative imagination and love. Venusian cypress trees are shown in the background.

Gold neckline and ornaments employ the solar forces. His belt indicates Time and the Zodiac, in the slanted circle of the ecliptic, written with the golden light of stellar forces.

The scepter combines a lunar crescent with the solar figure 8; his dominion results from a blend of their powers. The development of will, using solar and lunar forces, have already brought down and solidified into forming a vehicle.

The Grail denotes his function of Receptivity-Will, and the gift of transmutation after earthly victories, lifting the consciousness to partake of spiritual life, and brought by the dove of peace.

On the front of the chariot is a shield with the Indian *lingamyoni*, a symbol of the union of positive and negative forces and the generating power of the universe.

Above it, a blue-winged globe depicts the sun god Ra, and the spiritual mind carried aloft by wings of aspiration; and the gold of solar rays which beam to earth through the blue atmosphere.

The square on his chest with three black T's show the limiting power of Saturn. The eight folds of his skirt with geomantic talismanic symbols show dominion over the terrestrial forces.

Chariot wheels of orange show the solar energy, which causes the revolving motion—together with the influence of Key 10 or Wheel of Jupiter (the planet exalted in Cancer). The wheels also relate to the whirlwinds of Fire in the vision of Ezekiel, and represent the orbits of the planets.

The Sphinxes, Mercy and Severity, represent the senses which are always posing riddles concerning the mysteries of Nature, their reports not always reliable. Here at rest, they are under control.

This Key also relates to the entire solar system as the Chariot of God, called Merkavah.

The Sphinx has several meanings. It is variously pictured with a human head and the body of an animal, the body usually of reverse gender from that of the head. A favored symbol was the lion, and Egyptian pharaohs sometimes wore the tail of a lioness or of a cow behind them to depict the dual totality of Being in one person. One meaning is that of a symbol of Unity amid the multiplicity of existence, of the four Elements, along with the Quintessence of Spirit represented by the human figure.

> *"He who conquers shall have this heritage, and I will be his God and he shall be my son." (Revelation 21:7)*

> The Bhagavad Gita says, *"The Self is the Rider in the chariot of the body, of which the senses are the horses, and the mind the reins."*

COLORING INSTRUCTIONS

Yellow: Background.

Green: Trees; grass; wreath under crown.

Blue: Stream; faces on shoulder (not crescents). Wings on front of chariot (not disk), of deeper blue. Canopy and panel behind rider of night-sky blue.

Amethyst: Band circling chalice stem, studded with rubies.

Gray: Chariot; pillars; wall before city.

Gold: Chalice; crown; edging of collar and breastplate; ornament in square on breastplate; disk between wings; belt, except figures; scepter in right hand (except lunar crescent at top).

Silver: Crescent on shoulders and on scepter; stars on canopy and back panel. Rim of chalice cup outlined in silver.

White: Dove; cuffs; buildings (except rooftops); shield on chariot; white sphinx. Headdresses of both sphinxes, and design on skirt is also white, but best leave unpainted.

Steel: Armor on arms (blue-gray).

Brass: Breastplate (greenish-yellow).

Blonde:	Hair.
Red:	Rooftops; jewels on chalice; symbol on shield in front of chariot.
Orange:	Wheels of chariot.

The color of Path 18 on the Tree of Life is orange-yellow.

Meditation

Cheth am I, the Fenced Enclosure
Standing as an atmospheric shell
To protect the inner growing Light of Self.

I fend off interference from without
Until Its splendor is full-grown,
Till it bursts forth, removing walls,
And starts to light the Way.

The victory I have won is conquest of the mind,
Which brings all Nature's Mysteries
To Initiates who are able to remain
Receptive as a chalice to the Will of God.

The Twenty-Two Keys—The Chariot: Key 7

STRENGTH   TETH

8

Number Eight: 8 is the number symbolizing Infinity and rhythmic vibration. Its form shows reciprocal action and reaction, balance, and the fact that all opposites are effects of a single cause.

Path of Wisdom 19. It is called the Intelligence of the Secret of Spiritual Activities, "Its influence deriving from the supreme blessing and the supernal Glory."

Letter T or Th, in Hebrew "Teth," meaning "snake," referring to the coiled serpent power.

The numerical value of the letter Teth is nine, the 9th letter in the Hebrew alphabet.

Function: This Key shows the subconscious mind uplifted and regenerated to the point of having gained control over lower elements through constructive suggestion. It has developed beyond the natural instinctive level of animal intelligence, through discipline.

Astrologically: This Key represents Leo, symbolized by the Lion, heart, backbone, and courage. The serpent and eagle are sometimes interchangeable as symbols for the same regenerative force.

SYMBOLOGY OF THE COLORS AND ELEMENTS

An ancient form of the letter Teth showed a serpent coiled around the Hebrew letter Tav, meaning "cross." Or, more literally, Teth was suggested by a circle enclosing a cross.

The yellow sky shows the mental background from which this subconscious activity stems. Yellow is the color associated with Leo.

Yellow hair shows radiant energy; the wreath of the Empress has now come into bloom.

The white robe shows the purified aspect of subconsciousness now attained.

The 8 overhead, like on Key 1, indicates that subconsciousness has achieved equality of function as the result of conscious mastery.

The chain of red roses draped like a figure 8 about her waist and the lion symbolizes the systematic linking of desires designed to achieve dominion over the lower nature, to "tame the beast." It can only be tamed with love—the red roses.

In alchemy the "green lion" symbolizes unmodified, unripened animal nature in man. The "red lion" (Mars force) is the same nature, when controlled by spiritual progression. The "gold lion" is the radiant energy also called the "old lion," because it has always been.

You tame this lion, or beast of your own vehicle, your desires and appetites, even your very cells, by changing your pattern of reactions, making them positive, courageous, and constructive. This lion then becomes your servant, his natural strength a great tool.

The open plain shows that the forces being controlled and worked with are those of nature rather than artificial implements of man's invention.

The mountains in the background intimate some attainment has been achieved.

Teth is drawn to look like a coiled snake. This coiled force is related to the kundalini, dormant in most persons. It becomes automatically active with spiritual development, but is dangerous in unready, inwardly uncleansed vehicles. Ever renewal is inferred by the shedding of skins like a snake, thus Infinity.

Jesus said, "Be ye wise as serpents and harmless as doves." In other words, be as clever as those who would beguile you, but with pure and spiritual intentions.

> *"As Moses lifted up the serpent in the wilderness, so must the Son of Man be lifted up, that whoever believes in him should not perish but have eternal life." (John 3:14-16)*

COLORING INSTRUCTIONS

Yellow:	Background; eyes of lion.
Green:	Foreground; foliage; rose leaves; and leaves in hair.
Violet:	Mountain in background, all across.
White:	Woman's dress; teeth of lion.
Blonde:	Woman's hair.
Red:	Lion: roses; flowers in hair.

The color of Path 19 on the Tree of Life is yellow.

Meditation

Teth is occultly termed the "snake,"
For the spiral solar Fire which is lifted up,
When man controls desire, converts to Strength,
And Wisdom's secrets are revealed.

The heart which was a ravening beast
Once tamed becomes a friend
With boundless energy directed to a better end,
And thus a worthy residence for God's own Love.

The Twenty-Two Keys—Strength: Key 8

The Hermit   Yod
9

Number Nine: 9 is a number of completion, fulfillment, attainment of goal. Qabalistically called Foundation. Three times three, or perfection of the number 3.

Path of Wisdom 20: It is called the Intelligence of Will, and "it forms all patterns and prepares each individual for demonstration of the existence of the primordial glory, through Primordial Wisdom."

Letter J, or Y, or I, in Hebrew "Yod," meaning "hand," as the open or creative hand. This letter resembles a flame in formation, and is the foundation of most Hebrew letters. It is the flame of spiritual energy present in all forms of Life Experience; its upper point represents Primal Will, the remainder Wisdom. It is the basis of the Chaldean, the Square Hebrew, or Flame Alphabet.

The numerical value of the letter Yod is ten, as 10th letter of the Hebrew alphabet.

Identity: The Hermit has climbed as far as a human can go on earth, the highest point of physical earth, where he unites with the divine, feet on earth, head in heaven.

Function: Touch is the function of this Key. The hand of man is sensitive to touch, and union with God is also a contact, similar to touch.

Astrologically: This Key represents the earth-sign Virgo, which rules the digestive tract. This is the virginity attained through reaching true inner purity, and self-giving service. Virgo is ruled by Mercury, and he shows the highest operation of the law begun with the Magician. Here Mercury, exalted in Virgo, reaches its highest state, for now the Magician has reached a point of losing "self" to identify with the I AM, the Inner Self.

SYMBOLOGY OF THE COLORS AND ELEMENTS

Behind him is the Darkness, a symbol of the Unknown and Unknowable. Its indigo color signifies the Akasha and Absolute, the Radiant Darkness, and the hidden, interior Primordial field of Divine Operation.

The lantern, his own Light which he bears, shows the six-pointed Star of David the Beloved, a symbol of Universal Love. Virgo is also the sixth sign of the zodiac, and a sign of service to others.

His Yod-shaped cap is blue to symbolize the activity of memory and the subconscious mind. He looks back whence he came, meditating as does the Cosmic Process itself, while helping those who follow.

His staff is a symbol of Will, of Fire, and of the serpent power which has helped motivate his climb.

The robe is of a gray color symbolizing the Wisdom which keeps him warm. The Divine Mysteries provide their own protection from the unprepared.

Snowy peaks show the apparent cold of those heights of attainment where few have trod, yet his solitude is not loneliness. Snow represents the congealed "water" of Mind-Stuff.

On the Tree of Life, he channels the Cosmic Memory from Chesed to the solar Tiphareth.

As the Creative Hand, he represents the Fashioner of Worlds, and the Wisdom which is Foundation of all Knowing even as Yod is the foundation of all letters, the combinations of which become the whole Circle of Being.

"I have no will but to do the Will of Him that sent me."
(John 5:30)

COLORING INSTRUCTIONS

Yellow:	Lantern rays between black lines.
Blue:	Cap.
Brown:	Staff and shoe.
Gray:	Robe (except white sleeves of undergarment) and foreground (except peaks).
White:	Hair, beard, right and left sleeves of undergarment, mountain peaks.
Gold:	Star.
Indigo:	Background. Indigo is a combination of deep blue, violet, and black. The scene depicts a night sky.

The color of Path 20 on the Tree of Life is yellow-green.

MEDITATION

*Yod is the great creative open Hand
That Stretcheth forth o'er the Unmanifest
And fashioneth the fiery words of Life.*

*Free of self-will or personal desire,
In service to the Nameless One,
He sheds on those who also seek the way
A blessing of that Light divine.*

*Willing to share the ageless wisdom he has gained,
He awaits with patience others who still climb.
His fingers of Light reach out to touch
The unknown Realm ahead,
Uniting that which is below with that Above.*

The Twenty-Two Keys—The Hermit: Key 9

Wheel of Fortune   Kaph

10

Number Ten: Here we have the 1 of Beginning, plus the in-between stage represented by Zero, or stepping up one flight to begin another cycle. A number of perfection and dominion.

Path of Wisdom 21: This Path is called "The Rewarding Intelligence of those who seek. It receives the Divine Influence, and distributes by its benediction to all existing things."

Letter K, in Hebrew "Kaph," means "hand of man" grasping, and comprehending. Having tightly grasped, it again gives. "To him that hath shall be given."

The numerical value of the letter Kaph is equivalent to 20 in the Hebrew alphabet.

Identity: The Wheel is a symbol of progress, of rotation, cycles, and seasons. Its orange color complements Jupiter's blue, to balance forces. Its rotation shows simultaneously the effect resulting from cause, both ascending and descending at the same time.

Function: Grasp and comprehension of the Law.

Astrologically: This Key is related to the "greater benefic," Jupiter, our largest planet. Its symbolic color is blue or purple.

SYMBOLOGY OF THE COLORS AND ELEMENTS

Its Direction is West, the time of sunset, harvest, and payday.

The blue background refers to the power of Jupiter meaning "sky-father," the ancient god of rain, thunder, and lightning. The electro-magnetic "rain," or circulation of basic "root-matter" with its inner fire, is the substance of physical form.

The four figures at the corners are described both in Revelation and in Ezekiel. They depict the four "fixed signs" and the four elements:

> The Lion – Leo, Fire
> The Eagle – Scorpio, Water
> The Man – Aquarius, Air
> The Bull – Taurus, Earth

The configuration of these figures also refers to the mystical "squaring of the circle."

ROTA, on the outer rim, is the Latin word for "wheel." This alternates with the Hebrew IHVH, or Yahweh, the Tetragrammaton of the Divine Name.

In the second circle are shown four symbols of alchemy. Below the T is the symbol for Mercury (consciousness); below A is the symbol for Sulphur (passion-activity); below O is the symbol for salt (inertia); and below R is the symbol for "dissolution" and the sign Aquarius.

In the third circle are 8 spokes showing universal energy—like an eight-pointed star, and the eight-spoked wheels on the robe of the Fool. This is also a symbol of Spirit and the Quintessence.

The Center is the pivot—really the first plane of Creation, the archetypal World. From thence it radiates on out to the outer rim of manifestation—to the Word, and the World of Action.

True Creation begins with an initial whirling motion in a vast expanse of Limitless Light. Motion is not alone circular, but also spiral.

The freest part of Creation is the closest to the Center one can reach.

The yellow serpent represents the Involution of radiant Cosmic energy —light vibration, and the descent of the serpent-power.

The red (or active) Hermanubis ascending on the other side shows Evolution of form and the average stage of present human development, not beyond the intellectual level. He depicts the Egyptian Hermanubis, human body with jackal head, who guided souls on their journeys through the underworld.

The Sphinx typifies perfect identification with the SELF, the highest attainment by Self-Realization, as coming through Self recollection (the blue of Memory). He also depicts the union of male and female forces and the development of higher senses. He is free of the Wheel of Karma, and merely watches while it turns beneath him.

His sword is a symbol of Air, and the Word, as well as correct discrimination. It shows the subtle forces of breath at work in Formation.

Ezekiel 1 mentions, "Their construction being as it were, a wheel within a wheel."

In the words of the Alchemist:

"But first, of these elements make thou rotation,
And into Water thine Earth turn first of all;
Then of thy Water make Air by levigation,
And Air make Fire, then Master will I thee call
Of all our secrets, great and small.
The Wheel of the Elements thou canst turnabout,
Truly conceiving our writings without doubt."

Keystone of the Tarot with Meditations

COLORING INSTRUCTIONS

Yellow: Serpent, eagle's eye, and lion's eyes.

Blue: Background, and Sphinx (except for headdress).

Brown: Animals; lion tawny-brown, mixed with yellow.

Orange: All of the wheel.

Gold: Sword handle.

Steel: Sword blade.

Gray: Clouds. Storm clouds gray with white edges, due to greater density of water at center.

Blonde: Man's hair, and eagle's beaks.

White: In headdress and clouds, as stated above; eye of Hermanubis.

Red: Hermanubis (jackal-headed figure), and eagle's tongue.

The color of Path 21 on the Tree of Life is violet.

MEDITATION

*Kaph is the skillful grasping hand
That comprehends and uses tools of power,
Through diligence prepared to gain a just reward.*

*Having learned to give, he now receives,
And thus more fully he may give again.*

*He's learned to gauge the cycles of the Spheres
And put himself in balance with the Whole.
Through harmony and knowledge of the Cosmic Way,
The fortunes of each plane he handles well.*

JUSTICE   LAMED
11   ל

Number Eleven: Key 11 shows two 1's, equal polarities in equilibrium. This is the middle number of the series from 0 to 21.

Path of Wisdom 22: This Path is called the Faithful Intelligence, wherein spiritual virtues are deposited and increased, until they pass to those dwelling under the shadow thereof. In Hebrew, "AMN" means Faith.

Letter L: In Hebrew, "Lamed" (pronounced law-med) means, as a noun, "ox-goad" and as a verb, "to teach." Its form has the appearance of a serpent uncoiled, in action.

The numerical value of the letter Lamed is equivalent to 30 in the Hebrew alphabet.

Function: Whereas Key 10 showed a grasp of the Law, Key 11 shows application of the same law. The Emperor laid down this Law, but Justice mediates it! And WORK, for the function of this Key is work and action.

Astrologically: This Key is related to Libra, seventh sign of the zodiac, ruled by Venus, whose symbol is the balanced scale.

SYMBOLOGY OF THE COLORS AND ELEMENTS

The yellow background refers to Air (Libra), and to the Life Breath (the Ox of Aleph), partially concealed behind the "veil," the Jupiterian violet drapes.

Her Crown is a golden-edged triple-figure, resembling the letter Shin of Key 20, showing manifestation of exalted serpent-power, and man's release from three dimensional interpretations.

Circle-and-Square emblem on front of crown, the idea carried over from Key 10, shows movement of Spirit within the field of form.

Indigo T-square on front of dress indicates exaltation of Saturn in Libra. Saturn is the power of limitation working through Karma, to make possible the manifestation of form.

Hilt of sword repeats this symbol of the T-square, forged in the golden metal of the Sun. Enlightenment exalts form.

The sword implies the element of Air and activity cutting through obstruction to eliminate and free from falseness. Again, the Word.

Its steel is the metal of Mars, complement of Venus, as the red color of her robe is also the color of Mars, energizing, among other things, the adrenals which Venus rules.

Venus rules Libra, the sign of this Key, its green color adorning cape and crown.

Balance pans of the scales are of gold to show that weighing and measuring are also manifestations of radiant solar energy.

Seven lines of equal length support the pans, depicting seven aspects of the Life-Power. Libra is also the seventh sign of the zodiac.

Justice is established by accurate weighing and measurement of factors involved.

Though we do not escape the results of past actions, we may change them as we weigh and strike a balance, using the sword to eliminate error.

This same Ox-goad is used in teaching, for "to teach" is another meaning of the word Lamed. One may teach through goading into right action or through arousing the desire to attain.

The Sanskrit word Karma literally means "deed." So while you are reaping the fruit of yesterday's deeds, select and sow twice as many desirable ones for tomorrow, to strike the desirable balance, and even go beyond toward epigenesis.

Karma is never fate, but action and the result of action.

The fruit of inaction is loss of function. Not all action is physical.

When St. Paul was en route to Damascus, Jesus called to him, "Saul, Saul, why do you persecute me? It hurts you to kick against the goads."

Perfect Justice may manifest no likes nor dislikes, no partiality, lest it tip the scales of balance, and no more be Justice. Cosmic Law is just as impartial.

BALANCE

Perfect balance brings about a state of equilibrium, a condition of rest or poise as when two agencies which counteract each other's effect upon a body become precisely equal.

When the balance pans reach a precisely symmetrical or bilateral arrangement, there is expressed the idea of active equilibrium or, that is, of opposing forces that balance each other in such a way as to create a higher, static form. The caduceus is another example of that.

The scale of balance is said to indicate equilibrium on both the psychic and cosmic planes, and in both the outward and inward aspects of being.

One of Libra's pans leans toward the desire nature attributed to Scorpio, while the other tends toward Virgo and sublimation. It is up to man himself to balance the opposite forces within his nature and to thus achieve inner harmony.

COLORING INSTRUCTIONS

Yellow:	Between curtains in background.
Blonde:	Hair.
Green:	Crown, except emblem and border; cape over shoulders.
Blue:	Sleeves, same blue as canopy in Key 7.
Indigo:	T on dress yoke.
Violet:	Curtains, except cords, tassels, and fringe; oval around neck; Veil connecting pillars of throne—a lighter shade of violet.
Gray:	Throne and dais.
Gold:	Balances; Sword hilt; Rings holding drapery cords; Outline of Crown.
Steel:	Blade of sword.
White:	Square on crown; Shoe; Panels beside T on chest.
Red:	Robe, except cape and sleeves; cords; tassels; and fringe of draperies. Circle in emblem on Crown.

The color of Path 22 on the Tree of Life is green.

MEDITATION

Lamed is the Ox-Goad of instruction
Prodding to activity the great Life-Urge
That drives one on to seek the Self.

From her central place of equilibrium
She justly measures all experience,
Allowing no least thought or touch of feeling
To taint or tip the scales of faultless gold.

She helps to neutralize misdeeds of Karmic past
Decreeing new and better work.
Her airy sword cleaves straight a middle way
And setteth all things right.

Suspended Man   Mem
12

Number Twelve: 12 is a number of completeness, as in the 12 disciples and 12 signs of the zodiac. Reversed, 12 becomes 21, number of the last Key.

Path of Wisdom 23: This Path is called the Stable Intelligence, "the source of consistence, or power of permanence, in all the numerations."

Letter M, in Hebrew "Mem," translates as "seas" or "water." It suggests Silence, and is one of the three Mother letters, the Element Water in its original state. In chemical processes, water acts as a catalyst to hold particles in suspension.

The numerical value of the letter Mem is equivalent to 40 in the Hebrew alphabet.

Function: This Key in no way refers to hanging or suspension in the physical sense, but to an about face in deed and thought.

Astrologically: This Key's association is Neptune, ruler of the deep.

SYMBOLOGY OF THE COLORS AND ELEMENTS

His Path is correctly named Stable Intelligence, for the stable foundation of his life is the invisible realm of Spirit.

As the Water of Life, Mem represents the womb of all being.

Keystone of the Tarot with Meditations

Gray background shows the blending of opposites, of Spirit and Matter, wisely. Having done this, he has arrived at a complete reversal of mind and action.

The "Gallows" is shaped like the letter Tav of Key 21 (the Administrative Intelligence), which directs the forces of the universe. Six branches lopped from each side intimate the twelve signs of the zodiac, or twelve aspects of personality. The living wood shows Cosmic life. Through self-limitation on a lower level, one gains freedom on the greater—to achieve the "Dance of Life" realized in Key 21.

Limitation brings concentration and specialization. Prolonging of specialization at the spiritual level helps one toward Samadhi, in which most bodily functions are suspended, when consciousness and health of the being, both inner and outer, are in balance with Reality.

Law of Reversal: By this law, one reverses misery, failure, and their like, to substitute their opposites of health and happiness—not alone by thinking, but by application of principles.

White rope: Symbolizes the means of suspension, by twisted spirals of Universal Energy, the Pure White Light.

Yellow shoes: One arrives at correct understanding through exercise of the Intellect.

Red hose: His running action and reason (originating in Key 4) are stilled by this reversal. Red symbolizes the fire element.

Blue jacket: Water element. Mind-substance stemming from Key 2.

Silver buttons, cross, and crescents refer also to Key 2, showing the reflective quality of the moon metal and the element water, the first mirror of Nature, which reflects things upside-down. Symbol:

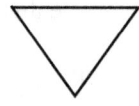

The pockets are containers of powers.

The 10 buttons are in number as the Spheres on the Tree of Life.

White hair indicates identity with the Ancient of Days.

Glory around head, illumination, shows him as embodiment of the One Light.

His vision and brain are active below the surface or ground level, where a place is hollowed out for the mind-stuff, or "water."

The Sanskrit word "mana" is a root word for "man," and the thinking mind.

> Yoga saying: *"When the Water of Mind-Stuff is perfectly clear, it mirrors the Light of the Spiritual Sun."*

> *"The Earth is the Lord's and the fullness thereof; the world and they that dwell therein. He has founded it upon the seas, and established it upon the floods."*

THE SUSPENDED MAN DEPENDS NOT ON THE EARTH BELOW HIM, BUT ON THAT WHICH IS ABOVE.

Keystone of the Tarot with Meditations

COLORING INSTRUCTIONS

Yellow: Shoes, and halo around head.

Blue: Coat, except ornaments.

Green: Grass.

Brown: Tree trunks, and slopes of earth.

Gray: Background.

Silver: Belt, buttons, pockets, and jacket edging.

White: Hair, and rope.

Red: Hose.

The color of Path 23 on the Tree of Life is blue.

MEDITATION

Mem is the Water and the Sea of Life,
The silent, primal, virgin Element
From which the worlds came forth,
Reflecting the glory of a committed goal.

To stabilize spiritual aims while yet on earth,
It seems one must walk upside down
To stand on heaven's floor.

But when true heaven is found within
Things right themselves so one may rise
Through higher planes, to the firm eternal Way.

TRANSITION

13

NUN

Number Thirteen: What seems as the "unluck" of 13 is only apparent, for all progress necessitates change and transformation.

Path of Wisdom 24: This Path is called the Imaginative Intelligence, or the "ground of similarity in the likeness of beings created after its aspects."

Letter N, in Hebrew "Nun," translates as "fish" when used as a noun. When used as a verb it translates to "sprout," or to "propagate," a prolific symbol.

The numerical value of the letter Nun is equivalent to 50 in the Hebrew alphabet.

Identity: The force represented here is also that of dissolution, which precedes every change or transformation. The last enemy to succumb is death, and to stop fearing change is one step in that direction.

Function: Fish were the first creatures with conscious life and the ability of locomotion, which is the function of this Key. In meditation, we angle for the "fishes" of spiritual revelation.

Astrologically: The attribution of this Key is Scorpio, ruled by Pluto, with Uranus exalted. Fixed water sign ruling death, generation, and inheritance.

SYMBOLOGY OF THE COLORS AND ELEMENTS

Nun (fish), the Hebrew letter of this Key, had a son called Joshua, which means in Hebrew "God liberates." He is the only Nun mentioned in the Bible. Joshua is a version of the same name as Jesus, with the same meaning (J H Sh V H). This is also the Tetragrammaton, the name of God JHVH, with Sh (fire) inserted in the middle. JHVH is inscribed on the inner garment of the Fool Key 0.

Red background refers to the Mars force of this former ruler of Scorpio. The power of life and growth belongs to those who obey its Law, but it is instrumental in death and destruction to those who disobey.

Two twists in the skeleton, at the Mars center above the pelvis and at the Venus center at the throat, a contortion physically impossible, refer to redirection of these energies on a higher non-physical level, to aid in attainment.

The bend in the river of consciousness shows the same thing, as it turns toward the rising Sun.

The seed at upper left refers to the Seed-Power of Scorpio's function. Two ovals, zeros, are united in this seed, and really are one. The inner oval represents the source of radiant energy from which proceed five rays: fire, air, earth, water, and ether. These extend to fill the space of the larger oval with energy of manifestation.

Zero also refers to the Fool Key, whose planet Uranus is exalted in Scorpio.

The white rose refers back to the same source, the Fool Key, showing purified desire and right motivation of the desire nature brought into unison with Primal Will.

He walks toward the South, from darkness of ignorance to the light of perfection; from the dark, disintegrative forces, toward the regenerative solar forces.

The sun rising in the East shows a cycle of new beginning and the dawn of higher consciousness.

Dark earth is the First Matter returned to its virginal state, the unknown.

The scythe is a conventional symbol for the Grim Reaper. Its T-shape refers to the coiled Kundalini force of the Saturn center at the base of the spine.

Its blade resembles a crescent, suggesting subconsciousness; steel is Mars' metal.

The male and female heads represent the rulership of the twin Spheres, and Abstract Deity, numbered two and three of the Supernals—Wisdom and Understanding—on the Tree of Life.

The boat represents the ark which has landed, with only the nucleus of a new beginning.

The wheel is the representation of progress, of new work to begin.

The boot shows where feet have trod, the water spilling out.

At death the seed, or nucleus of Self, is expelled from the physical form. The true part of us is deathless and eternal, taking on new form, for the soul demands new experience.

> *"You have taken Wisdom as your guide in everything, and called Understanding your mother. That is why I have given this revelation to you; there is a reward in store for you with the Most High..." (11 Esdras)*

> Paul said, *"We shall not all die, but we shall all be changed in a flash."*

COLORING INSTRUCTIONS

Yellow: Sun, band on man's crown.

Blue: Stream.

Green: Rosebush and foliage.

Brown: Handle of scythe, hair of man (light brown).

Steel: Blade of scythe (blue-gray).

Gray: Boat, wheel, and shoe.

White: Skeleton and rose. Seed is unpainted.

Blonde: Woman's hair.

Gold: Points in crown worn by man. Fish in stream.

Red: Sky in background.

The color of Path 24 on the Tree of Life is blue-green.

MEDITATION

From the deep Waters of Mem is drawn the Fish,
Called Nun, the secret Wisdom of the One.
Symbol of generation and immortality.
Things ever change yet stay perpetually the same.

The ark that's carried safe across the flood,
The soul that has survived travail,
Has found a place to rest on firmer ground
Where seed and harvest may again abound,
And Adam's error stripped away, the cleansed one
Is given fresh beginnings in a Newer Day.

Temperance

Samekh

14

Number Fourteen: 14 is the Knowledge of Conversation of the Holy Guardian Angel and tempering metal-mettle by fire and water. Nature alone does not perform this activity; it requires the intervention of higher powers, when ready.

Path of Wisdom 25: This Path is called the Intelligence of Probation and Trial, "the first temptation by which God tests the devout, or the compassionate."

Letter S, or soft C: In Hebrew "Samekh" means "prop" or "tent peg," the support of a dwelling place. In formation, it is likened to a serpent which has completed the cycle of its action and swallowed its tail, now in perfect control of the serpent force. See Key 8 Strength and Key 11 Justice.

The numerical value of the letter Samekh is equivalent to 60 in the Hebrew alphabet.

Identity: Purification must be done by the Higher Self, or the Holy Guardian Angel. While sometimes terrifying to the impure, the product of Temperance is the gold of enlightenment.

Function: The rainbow is caused by rays of Sun shining through raindrops or mist. Fire and water acting upon each other is one of the functions of this Key, as symbols of tempering metal.

Astrologically: The letter Samekh correlates with the fire-sign Sagittarius.

SYMBOLOGY OF THE COLORS AND ELEMENTS

The gold background refers to solar energies coming to earth from life-giving Sun, the rays of the physical Sun.

Michael, meaning "one who is like God," is the archangel of the Sun, here identified by the solar disk on his head.

A rainbow represents the water of consciousness mingling with solar energy—vibrations of One Light refracting into differentiations of color, as sun dries the waters of the flood.

The same Hebrew word is used for both Sagittarius and for rainbow *Qesheth* (a bow). The angel's fiery wings combine fiery-red with water blue.

The rainbow appears to form a natural bridge between heaven and earth, and it was thought by primitive peoples that when a rainbow appeared in the sky, God was seeking to make contact with man, providing a bow for man's arrow of aspiration.

In the Hebrew religion, it formed a sign of the covenant of God's promise to man, involving His pardon and reconciliation with the human race.

Christian art sometimes depicts the rainbow as a throne of the Christ, particularly in representations of the Last Judgment. Its overall symbology is that of union, of a link between heaven and earth, God and man, sent from above.

Wrath is the quality associated with this Key, and the Hebrew word for "wrath" relates more to quivering, or vibration. Vibration is the activity which makes both sight and manifestation possible.

At the neckline of the robe, which is white for purity, are seen the letters IHVH, the Tetragrammaton, Yahweh. On its front is shown the seven-pointed star of Mastery and of Venus.

The Vase of Art refers to the vessel of human personality, "Our Mercury" of the alchemist, and the furnace in which the purification takes place, to rid the aspirant of error.

The Vase's orange color refers both to the Sun and to Gemini, as the habitation of Mercury.

Water represents the Astral fluid or subconscious activities at work, to modify the animal nature shown here by the earthy color.

The lion is of the fire element, as opposites are tested against each other.

The eagle, of the water element, is modified in turn by fire, falling in five Yods or five differentiations as shown by the five elements: ether, fire, air, earth, and water.

Between the twin peaks of Wisdom and Understanding rises the Path of Return to God—the Path which began at the pool.

The Crown shown above the peaks is the one given to him who overcomes or attains, gaining self-mastery and union with the One Self.

Truth is established by Trial, that is, doing something about what you have learned.

> *"Never again shall all flesh be cut off by the waters of the flood. I shall set my bow in the cloud, and it shall be a sign of the covenant between me and the earth." (Genesis 9:11)*

> *"I saw a mighty angel with a rainbow over his head." (Revelation 10:1)*

COLORING INSTRUCTIONS

Yellow: Path to mountain; crown over mountain peaks; yods over eagle; torch flame, streaked with red. Eyes of lion.

Brown: Handle of torch.

Blue: Water in pool, and stream from vase. Highlights of wings.

Green: Grass.

Orange: Vase; disk on head of angel

Violet: Mountains (dilute).

Gold: Background area; star on gown. (Or substitute yellow, with a touch of orange.)

White: Dress; eagle; top of lion's head.

Blonde: Angel's hair; beak, feet, and legs of eagle.

Red: Angel's wings, with blue highlights; Lion; Top of eagle's head.

Rainbow colors: The rainbow begins on the inside with violet, and continues with succeeding bands of color of indigo, blue, green, yellow, orange, and red, in that order.

The color of Path 25 on the Tree of Life is blue.

MEDITATION

Samekh, I'm called, a tent peg or a prop,
That which supports foundations of a house
And nails things down to stabilize the whole.

Michael, fiery archangel of the Sun,
Has been sent from Above
To test and prove the seeker's readiness.

Through trial by fire of opposites,
Resistance from "unlike" arousing heat,
The raw gold melts within its crucible.
Purging to purify and to refine,
He makes firm the foundation of the soul.

The Deceiver Ayin
15

Number Fifteen: 15 is about bondage and the delusion of outer appearances. This Key is called the First Stage of Spiritual Unfoldment.

Path of Wisdom 26: This Path is called the "Renewing Intelligence, whereby God reneweth All, which are begun afresh, in the creation of the world."

Letter O, in Hebrew "Ayin," means "eye," or "outward appearance," or "fountain."

The numerical value of the letter Ayin is equivalent to 70 in the Hebrew alphabet.

Identity: For the one who has been tempered and tried in the previous Key 14 Temperance, this Key is the first step to seeing squarely the ridiculousness of all that had appeared before as "most important, in the eyes of the worldly consciousness."

Function: Its function is Mirth—incongruity causing laughter, which is a cleansing agent.

Astrologically: This is Capricorn, ruled by Saturn. Physically it rules the knees, to which we are brought in prayer when afflicted.

SYMBOLOGY OF THE COLORS AND ELEMENTS

The black background represents the darkness of ignorance and the veil hiding Truth.

Bat wings symbolize a creature of night and darkness, and of the air.

The figure of a winged goat as used in Ancient Middle Eastern teachings has since degenerated from a valid symbol of a Teacher to that used in witchcraft as their god, Satan.

The goat of Capricorn is caricatured, in its negative sense of earthy-brown sensuality. Do not underrate the sign itself: in Capricorn are traditionally born the World Saviors, just past the winter's longest and darkest night, as the darkness just before the dawn, spiritually too.

Inverted pentagram shows mental delusion in belief that man is still dominated by earthly elements, before he learns what he is.

The red eyes correlate with Mars' exaltation in Capricorn, ruling Aries. Eyes deceive, and the devil is called the father of lies.

The pedestal is only a front, intended to show a cube which has no depth and is not even real. It shows that partial sight is all that is possessed by those who accept surface appearances, for physical vision reveals only a fraction of what is there.

On his uplifted hand is the symbol of Saturn, planet of limitation and discipline. He shows the whole palm in an effort to deceive others into believing that there is nothing except as physically seen, that he's showing you all that exists. This is contrary to the hand of Key 5 The Teacher, which illustrates all you see is not all that there is.

The symbol at the navel is an adaptation of Mercury, the red cross of physical response to mental activity. It is an imperfect symbol.

The torch smolders wastefully showing the inverted use of the Mars force, as does the tail of the man which it activates.

The tail of the woman suggests the outgrowth of forbidden fruit, or the fruits of misdirected action. Both their tails point to over development of the animal nature.

The horns also show their descent in consciousness through baser living—Adam and Eve at the lowest stage since their fall.

The intelligence on their faces shows that they will not remain in bondage to appearances. Once these two laugh at their troubles, they will just fade away, like a nightmare fades at dawn.

The tempter came to Jesus, after he was baptized and spent 40 days fasting in the wilderness, to see if he would turn aside to enjoy an earthly kingdom. Each must overcome some hurdle or other, past the dweller on his particular threshold, before he is proven ready to scale spiritual heights.

This has to be the first step out on the spiritual path, after all the preparation, because your strength must be tried before you have gone too far; that the fall, if any, will not be too great.

When attainment comes, the devil shall be cast into the fire of the Lake of Divine Understanding.

This occurs as the individual casts his own negative tendencies into the fire, along with outgrown encumbrances of his past. Huge empty bundles of anxiety, needless burdensome attachments, negative emotions, all are tossed into the consuming flame.

As they disintegrate, the devil, which they perpetuated, dissolves with them and man moves out, free to rise in consciousness. The encumbrances that have bound his feet to earthly clay are gone, along with the impostor, so man is free to serve his true Lord.

Keystone of the Tarot with Meditations

> *"And the great dragon was cast out, that old serpent called the devil and Satan, which deceiveth the whole world. He was cast out into the earth, and his angels were cast out with him,"* fighting Michael and his angels of Light. (Revelation 12:9)

COLORING INSTRUCTIONS

Yellow: Upper half of insignia near devil's navel. Hair of man and woman is yellow streaked with red, as is the torch flame, and flames on tail of man.

Green: Tail of woman.

Brown: Torch handle; foreground. Body and wings of devil are a grayed brown.

White: Beard; horns of man and woman; star.

Gray: Puffs of smoke below torch.

Steel: Rings and chains.

Red: Cross on devil's navel; grapes on tail of woman; devil's eyes; highlights in flames.

The color of Path 26 on the Tree of Life is blue-violet.

MEDITATION

Ayin is the Eye that uses sleight-of-hand,
Whose tricks make things appear what they are not.
He covers unsavory wares with wrappers of allure
To tempt desires and coarsen senses on a downward trend.

But their apparent enslavement is but illusion.
When the captives have grown wise with trust in God
They can easily lift the loose chains off, and laugh
At caricatures and cheap veneer that brought them there.

Then may they understand why the Threshold of Divine Reality
Is guarded from admitting those not yet prepared
Who wait awhile outside the Stable Door, but not alone:
For God is there, the Lord of darkness as of light,
And out of darkness comes the Light.

The Tower

16

Peh

Key Sixteen: 16 is the Second step of Spiritual Unfoldment dealing with Spiritual Awakening.

Path of Wisdom 27: This Path is called the "Natural or Exciting Intelligence. Through it is consummated and perfected the nature of every existent being under the orb of the sun, in perfection."

Letter P, F, or Ph: In Hebrew, "Peh," means "mouth," when used as the organ of speech.

The numerical value of the letter Peh is equivalent to 80 in the Hebrew alphabet.

Identity: The occult force here symbolized as a bolt of lightning is the basis of inner modifications of the personal vehicle which result in enlightenment.

Function: A glimpse of the Sun flashes from out of the ignorance of the veiled unknown, bringing the impact of the Christ force, shown as lightning. Herewith comes the first perception of Truth.

Astrologically: This is the planet Mars, whose color red indicates its fiery nature.

SYMBOLOGY OF THE COLORS AND ELEMENTS

Its blinding flash removes the worldly viewpoint so drastically as to seem at first terrible, breaking down all the crystallizations of erroneous belief and accumulated conditions from the past, and removing the scales from one's vision.

Yet this awakening is wonderful in that it ends the dream of separation from God, and brings one near to the Path of Return. By leveling the false edifice of self-separation, it makes way for the better Way.

The crown is a false one, representing material achievement; it is the usurper's crown of self-will, representing a false kingdom that declares matter and form as its gods.

Both the conscious mind (the man) and subconscious mind (the woman) must readjust to the Truth, having been clothed in the unfitting garments of concealment, and crowned with false knowledge.

The crown is an emblem of victory and distinction, while the tower shows a rise above the common level, somewhat as a ladder rises up from the ground. But that which is founded on earthly premise must come down, the material crown cast off when the real King speaks! The wild pursuit of selfish and egotistical ideas comes to naught, and small-mindedness cannot hold the grandeur of the Sun.

Like the Holy Spirit descending on the Apostles, the 22 yods (each a letter/word in the Hebrew alphabet) fall as tongues of fire, representing the 22 Living Yods of the Spirit of the Word. This is in opposition to the 22 levels of man-made brick (not stone) which comprise the tower, here representing the "letter of the word." *"For the letter killeth, but the Spirit giveth life."* (2 Corinthians 3:6)

The yods at left are a "seeded" figure eight, or double hexagon. The yods at right are shaped like the Tree of Life.

The arrow-head shape of the lightning bolt resembles an ancient symbol for Beth (house). "Except the Lord build the house, he labors in vain that buildeth it."

The building constructed of human error and ignorance, desecrated by wrong words and thoughts, must fall.

The athanor, or alchemists' furnace, was shown as a tower to indicate that the metamorphosis of matter implies ascent as well. Windows near the top correspond to the eyes and mind of man. Flesh-colored, or traditional gray, bricks denote the image of a human being. Its vertical structure denotes elevation and evolution.

The tongue, Mars-like, is aggressive. Though rash speech can be destructive, words rightly-directed carry the power of creation.

The letter Peh is formed like a letter Kaph, with a tongue inserted.

The Tower of Babel also had to do with using speech to gain a way to heaven, or to force a physical entrance to a spiritual realm.

While the Tower was built on a physical foundation of brown, the color of the devil's appearance-geared world, the Yods and falling figures must now depend on a superior foundation, not based on earth.

An old alchemical statement goes: "Gold cometh from the North." Here is the Fire. In comparing this with the previous Key 15 it takes a nightmare to wake us up, at first.

The direction North is assigned to this entire Key, and the idea of North to all the dark pillars of the Tarot series, because North is the place of the absence of sun.

"As the lightning comes from the East, and shines as far as the West, so will be the coming of the Son of Man." (Matthew 24:27)

"Not what goes into the mouth defiles a man, but what comes out of the mouth—this defiles a man." (Matthew 15:11)

COLORING INSTRUCTIONS

Yellow:	Star. Rope-like bands on crown, woman's crown. Yods are yellow with a small yod-shaped red tongue in lower right corner of each. Small part of flames is yellow.
Blue:	Woman's dress, and man's hose.
Gold:	Lightning flash; crown (except rope bands).
Gray:	Storm clouds, gray with white edges. (See "flesh"—tower.)
Brown:	Cliff, grayed-brown; top a lighter shade.
Blonde:	Hair of woman
Flesh:	Tower to represent the human body as the house of God. (Traditional light gray may be used, if you prefer.)
Red:	Coat, and boots of man, and shoes of woman. Flames are mostly red, with a little yellow.

The color of Path 27 on the Tree of Life is red.

MEDITATION

Peh is the Mouth which thunders Truth
Through an opening rent by lightning flash.
The man-made structure that seemed strong before
Proves flimsy now before the Strength and Word of God.

Ten tongues flash forth with the Creative Word,
And twelve more speak of human personality.

One does not reach God by towers built from earth,
But heaven sends down a ladder of its own,
Built out of Fire, and Power, and the Holy Word,
For the aspiring one to climb up on.

The Star   Tzaddi
17

Key Seventeen: 17 represents the third stage of Spiritual Unfoldment dealing with Meditation and Revelation.

Path of Wisdom 28: This Path is called the Natural, or Active, Intelligence: "Thence is created the spirit of every creature of the supreme orb, and the activity or motion to which they are subject."

Letter Tz, Ts, or Cz. In Hebrew "Tzaddi," means "fishhook," a tool for angling.

The numerical value of the letter Tzaddi is equivalent to 90 in the Hebrew alphabet.

Identity: The woman is Isis-Urania, or unveiled Truth—the veil of ignorance removed in rare moments of revelation through meditation. Man cannot unveil her. Only those prepared to behold Reality can discern Truth.

Function: The function of this Key is finding the Truth through Meditation and Revelation.

Astrologically: This Key's ruling sign is Aquarius, ruler of stars and the heavens. Its symbol is the same one used for alchemical dissolution, or the reducing of substance to its primal matter. It also rules electricity and lightning. This Key's ruling planets are Saturn and Uranus.

SYMBOLOGY OF THE COLORS AND ELEMENTS

Uranus is also the planet of Key 0, the Fool. Violet on the color scale refers to the sign Aquarius. "Ye shall know the Truth, and the Truth shall make you free."

The background is blue, for the starlit night holds no more darkness. On the contrary, after the Awakening, Truth begins to reveal itself.

The Central Star is symbolic of solar energy, concentrated and radiated from all in the universe. All the stars are 8-pointed to show the power of radiant energy. The secondary half-points or budding potential of the large Star will be fully developed in Key 19.

The smaller stars represent the planets, or the seven different energies of the chakras.

A red ibis, or fishing bird, relates to the meaning of the letter Tzaddi. It is an Egyptian Bird, sacred to Hermes, or Mercury. In meditation one baits a hook to search the "waters" of universal subconsciousness.

The "seas" of Mem, Key 12, provides a field of operation for Tzaddi, fishhook.

In fishing, one must first silence the superficial activity of the thinking processes, which, however, supervise the activity like the ibis.

The tree, by its shape, represents the brain and nervous centers.

She kneels partially on the firm foundation of facts, of earth; the other foot rests firmly on the foundation of the subconscious mind.

The two vases stand for the self-conscious mind and the subconscious mind. Ellipses are zeros, for No-Thing. The stream flowing from these is used to stir up the Greater Subconscious Mind. The stream on land falls into five parts for purification of the five physical senses. She lifts the vases.

The mountain, colored violet for Aquarius, shows perfection of the Great Work and final achievement of alchemical practice.

Meditation is the safest method of regeneration, drawing up nerve force from the chakra centers without direct concentration on them.

"We have seen his Star in the East." The Star of meditation directs us to the birth of the Christ child within ourselves.

Keystone of the Tarot with Meditations

COLORING INSTRUCTIONS

Yellow: Large central Star.

Green: Grass and leaves of tree.

Blue: Background, water in pool and pouring from vases; ovals of vases and stripe around necks of deeper blue.

Violet: Mountain range and foothills.

Orange: Vases (except stripes, ovals, and handles).

Flesh: Body.

White: Seven smaller stars, vase and top stripe across oval on vase at your right, lower stripe on vase at left, highlights on water.

Brown: Tree trunk.

Blonde: Hair.

Red: Bird. Top band over oval on vase at left of picture. Lower band over oval on vase at right.

Gold Ink: If desired, outline with pen inside large star; lightning streak and 7 pointed rays from white planets; highlights on water.

The color of Path 28 on Tree of Life is violet.

The Twenty-Two Keys—The Star: Key 17

MEDITATION

Tzaddi, the heavenly Fish Hook, who abides
As Mother of all, above the firmament,
Dips up the golden Waters of Life
To draw the hidden Fish out from its depths,
And gather, one by one, the human soul
Unto that finer realm of Light.

When falseness has been stripped away
Through trials refining that which came before,
The higher Truth can be revealed.
Then when the mouth of man is silent,
The Voice of heaven speaks
And seven stars within himself
Are kindled from the greater Sun.

THE MOON

QOPH

18

Key Eighteen: 18 is the fourth stage of Spiritual Unfoldment. In this stage takes place the alchemical transformation of the natural vehicle to one of sensitive refinement, responsive to higher forces.

Path of Wisdom 29: This Path is called the Corporeal Intelligence, or Body Consciousness. "It informs every body which is incorporated under all orbs, and is the growth thereof."

Letter Q, in Hebrew "Qoph," means "back of head." The earliest form of Qoph was like a knot, and the letter Q often resembles such. This letter precedes or prepares the way for the next letter Resh, which means "head."

The numerical value of the letter Qoph is equivalent to 100 in the Hebrew alphabet.

Identity: Subconscious powers are represented by the Moon, on this Path of Return.

Function: The function of this Key is Sleep and Organization. This is the stage of development when bodily forces become fully organized.

Astrologically: This Key is related to the sign Pisces and the planets Jupiter and Neptune.

SYMBOLOGY OF THE COLORS AND ELEMENTS

The blue distance shows planes of consciousness we may enter after the body has changed.

The moon has 16 principal rays and 16 short ones, which refer to the 32 Paths of Wisdom, or 32 modes of human conscious energy, woven together to make human personality and bodily vesture, referred to as the Tree of Life.

The path is narrow, showing the requirement of concentration on the goal. Cycles and rhythm, waxing and waning, ups and downs, are shown by its undulation. Yet it ever rises. Beginning in the realm of the familiar, the cultivated area of experience, it passes from less-known to Unknown; yet it is a path marked by the footsteps of those who have gone before. It is the Path of Return to God.

The mountains beyond are also the Source. The way of attainment is the Path of Return to the heights of identity with the One Reality.

The Towers show mental attitude of the average man, self-protection against his environment; also the outposts of things known. The windows symbolize correct reasoning which admits a little light. But these towers represent the ordinary limits to human perception and sensation. They are not boundaries, but portals to the Beyond.

18 Yods show the descent of Life-Force from above, into conditions of bodily existence. These combine a yellow color, solar energy, with red, for the vital force in blood. Powers of the subconscious mind develop through changes in the chemical constitution of blood.

The dog and wolf are both of the canine family, the wolf through natural evolution, and the dog through human adaptation; the one is a symbol of Nature, the other of the modification of Nature through Art. They represent the trained and untrained intellect.

The scarab beetle is an Egyptian sacred symbol representing the immortality and evolution of the soul, rolling before him the emblem of the sun.

The crayfish is a little lower form of life, the crustacean—his shell of self-separation, like undeveloped man. It suggests instinctive energy, and the force of Scorpio. He is the great Fish, pulled up from the astral waters—the soul in the process of being reborn in God.

Plants and Stones: are a still lower form of life and manifestation.

Pool: This is the reduced essential from which all things once again emerge.

The body is built and maintained by the automatic consciousness. When man is ready fully to return to God, his vehicle must be further refined, and made a vessel fully capable to accept the Light of Christ.

The Moon accomplishes in one month its circle around the earth, comparable to the circle of earth around the Sun, which requires one year. Thus is the month a reflection of the solar year, as moonlight itself is a reflection of sunlight.

The most obvious effect of the lunar cycle is upon the watery tides and upon the female biological functions. The moon has long been designated as ruler over water and woman, and is also said to be related to the soul and the astral plane.

Measures of time were first equated with lunar rhythms before solar timing, because of the easily observable increase and decrease of the lunar crescent. At each New Moon, for three nights the moon disappears from the heavens, but on the fourth day it reappears, or is "reborn."

Certain people taught that the soul journeys to the moon immediately after death, which equates it again with the astral level. "This day you shall be with me in paradise." (Luke 23:43)

"When deep sleep falleth upon man, in slumberings upon the bed, then He openeth the ears of men, and sealeth their instruction." (Job 33)

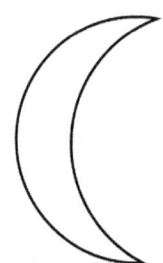

COLORING INSTRUCTIONS

Yellow:	Path, Moon and rays; Yods, except yod-shaped tongue of flame at lower right corner of each larger yod.
Green:	Grass in foreground, which ends before reaching towers.
Gray-green:	Scarab beetle.
Blue:	Sky background and pool.
Gold:	Solar disk carried by scarab.
Gray:	Towers; stones beside pool; wolf.
Violet:	Crawfish; mountains (a diluted violet).
Brown:	Dog; plains between grass and mountains.
White:	Highlights on pool; teeth of wolf.
Red:	Flames in yods (see yellow).

The color of Path 29 on the Tree of Life is violet-red.

MEDITATION

Qoph is the "back of the head"
Where is concealed the working place
Of mystic temple builders who perform,
Even in sleep, the "white work" of the Moon.

By her allure the seeking soul is drawn
To journey on the Path from depths to heights.
Threading the world past opposites,
It passes through the needle's eye
Returning regenerated Man to God.

The Sun
19

Resh

Key Nineteen: 19 is the Fifth Stage of Spiritual Unfoldment. It represents New Birth from natural into spiritual humanity.

Path of Wisdom 30 is known as the Collective Intelligence—"thence astrologers, by the judgment of stars and heavenly signs derive their speculations, and the perfection of their science, according to the motions of the stars."

Letter R, in Hebrew "Resh," means "head," "face," or "countenance." In the head are gathered together, or collected, the human powers of authority and leadership.

The numerical value of the letter Resh is equivalent to 200 in the Hebrew alphabet.

Identity: The Sun of our solar system collects and distributes power impulses, which hold all together. Behind it is the Spiritual Sun, which was glimpsed behind the Fool—the Life-Power as the essence from which all was created.

Function: Regeneration, which is also called the Directing Principle.

Astrologically: The ruler of this Key is the Sun, whose metal is gold. It is the center of our solar system, and ruler of the sign Leo.

SYMBOLOGY OF THE COLORS AND ELEMENTS

The Sun is the symbol used for "alchemical gold," and the subject of the Great Work. This living radiance performs transformations in both vehicle/body and consciousness.

Sun worship has been widely practiced in ancient times, having reached its most advanced form, so far as now known, in Mexico and Peru. Even Rome permitted Mithraic solar cults during the days of its Empire.

The Sun in these cults was usually equated with a hero image, in contrast to the concept of a Father God who ruled the heavens.

Some saw the Sun as the Eye of the Supreme God, and not only as the source of heat and light, but of supreme riches, whose golden drops rain down on those below, when the opaque crust of the senses has been rendered sufficiently transparent so they may receive them, a function performed by the Sun in its purifying aspect.

The human features depict the Sun as a symbol of living, conscious intelligence—a Being, rather than a thing. All celestial bodies, say ancient doctrines, are vehicles of intelligence. The Moon shows some things through reflected light, the Sun with direct Light.

The short rays shown in the Star of Key 17 have here extended to wavy lines of equal length, and show the development of the female potential.

The small lines drawn within the Sun's circle usually number 125, as cube of the number 5, to indicate dominion of Spirit over matter.

The 13 orange Yods falling down from the Sun indicate the energies of the Hermit Key 9 in his secret activity, with a tinge of Mars (yellow plus red). The Yods also depict Unity and Love, by their placement, two sets of sixes (The Lovers Key 6), plus an extra Yod between, showing a spiritual fire.

Five sunflowers, four of them open, indicate four stages of evolution in form: mineral, animal, vegetable, and human, plus the fifth stage of spiritual, regenerated humanity, not yet fully developed. This fifth flower has turned its face toward the Sun above.

The five rows of stones in the wall are of true stone, showing God's work, and indicating the esoteric meaning of the word "stone," in Hebrew *ehben*, which is the union of Father and Son. The five rows indicate that the information drawn from the reports of the five senses are of use as far as they go.

But the children have turned their backs upon this, having "outgrown" the limited perspective of physical life alone. They are the new-born regenerated conscious and subconscious minds, and personality.

The sundial, which tells time by the light of the Sun, is also behind them, for Time itself has earthly limitations.

They face outward toward a freer way for which they have been trained. This is a high stage of development where one becomes a true channel for the One Divine Will, having given up his own petty way.

This is a degree of adeptship, yet not complete. They have the joy of new-found freedom in Truth and in being filled with the Light of Christ, the Son. They have themselves become new Sons of God.

The flowers symbolize Life, and the wall symbolizes Word, as the "enclosure of speech."

> *"Except ye become as a little child, ye shall in no wise enter the Kingdom of Heaven." (Matthew 18:3)*

> *"Unto you that fear My Name, the Sun of Righteousness shall rise, with healing in his wings." (Malachi 4:2)*

Keystone of the Tarot with Meditations

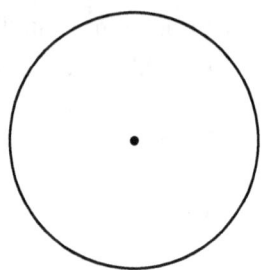

COLORING INSTRUCTIONS

Yellow: Sun and its rays; sunflower petals, and face of sundial.

Green: Leaves; grass (circle darker than other grass).

Blue: Background, encircling the rays extending from the Sun.

Brown: Sunflower centers.

Gray: (Light gray.) Wall, and sundial, except face.

Orange: Yods.

Blonde: Hair.

The color of Path 30 on the Tree of Life is orange.

MEDITATION

Resh am I, the Countenance and Head
Which brings to you the glory of the Sun
And melts away all darkness with the Light.

When a chick matures within its tiny world,
And the shell is broken, with great joy
He finds himself all-new in wider realms,
So man, when heaven nears and Greater Ones approach,
Finds himself as a little Child upon the Way,
Eager to gain true Wisdom of Reality.

Judgement

20

Shin

Key Twenty: 20 is the Sixth Stage of Spiritual Unfoldment showing human consciousness on the verge of blending with the Universal Consciousness.

Path of Wisdom 31 is called Perpetual Intelligence, because it rules the movements of the Sun and the Moon, according to their constitution, and causes each to gravitate in its respective orb.

Letter Sh, in Hebrew "Shin," means "tooth," suggesting a serpent's fang. It is called the Holy Letter, and one of the three Mother Letters, the one for Fire. As a tooth, it breaks down all form in readiness to start over. Also called "Life Breath of the Divine Ones."

The numerical value of the letter Shin is equivalent to 300 in the Hebrew alphabet.

Identity: This is Judgement Day, when Spirit shall judge the earth.

Function: The function of this Key is Realization.

Astrologically: This Key correlates with Pluto, and with Vulcan, both of which are associated with Fire.

SYMBOLOGY OF THE COLORS AND ELEMENTS

The angel shown is Gabriel, called Archangel of the Moon, the reflective quality of Universal Memory. His name translated means Might of God, or "Strength of God."

The cloud is shown as a circle, containing a figure 8, to suggest eternity as well as the fourth dimension. Clouds surround the angel because the true nature of Self is veiled by the substance of appearances.

12 rays of Light of True Self pierce the cloud—Gabriel is one aspect of that Light.

7 rays descend from the trumpet, seven great sounds whose vibrations help wake the spiritual centers.

The trumpet represents specialization of the Life Breath in sound. It calls forth certain subconscious activities which result in final liberation. Correctness of sound is important in music as well. To choose harmonies of refinement is a requirement upon the spiritual path.

Red wings to indicate active energy of the Fire element are assigned to this Key. "Hear thou the Voice of the Fire," says a Chaldean oracle.

The banner shows the magic square of Mars—its equal-armed cross relating to Key 4 and the fourth dimension. Mars also belongs to the Fire element.

The icebergs refer to the alchemical process called "fixing the volatile." When we arrest the stream of consciousness and make it solid, we are emancipated from illusion. The higher consciousness, as in Key 12 Suspended Man, arrests the flow of mental energy. The sea is the end of flowing water, begun with the High Priestess. Her work is completed.

The child of earth has risen from the grave of error. As the first destruction was by Water, the second is by Fire—Spirit in Judgement.

The stone coffins supported by the sea show this mental substance as the support of form. Their solidity suggests three-dimensional form, while bodies standing at right angles suggest the fourth dimension.

The gray color of their skin indicates that they have overcome earth's limited concepts, and have overcome all pairs of opposites. They function on the astral plane, their attitude reversed from that of earth—the man passive and the woman active in attitude.

Their arms are lifted in the formation of the letters LVX, which spell "Light" in Latin.

Fire has been called an overstate of matter, having the highest vibration among the "Four Elements," or principles of Nature. Being more mysterious in aspect and origin, it is sometimes referred to as the "Eye of God."

Fire being least dense among the four phases of Matter, it manifests both visibly and invisibly—the discernible and substantial flame comparable to the indiscernible ethereal or spiritual flame. Spiritual Fire has the quality of Light.

> Gabriel appeared to Daniel, saying, *"Understand,*
> *O Son of Man, that the vision is for the end of Time."*
> (Daniel 8:17)

COLORING INSTRUCTIONS

Yellow — Inside trumpet bell; rays from clouds.

Blue: — Upper background; water; angel's dress (darker blue).

Gray: — Human bodies; coffins of darker gray.

White: — Clouds; banner, except cross; icebergs, white with delicate blue highlights; collar edging on dress of angel.

Gold: — Trumpet outside.

Blonde: — Hair of angel, woman, and child.

Red: — Cross on banner; angel's wings.

Brown: — Hair of man.

The color of Path 31 on the Tree of Life is red.

MEDITATION

*I am the fiery Tooth called Shin
That biteth through all barriers
Reducing to essential elements
That which is to be transformed
And used for higher purposes.*

*With me comes Gabriel, whose flag proclaims
Swift action and great Might.
Calling forth children of the Light,
He bids the sleeping ones to rise
And complete the cycle of the Work.*

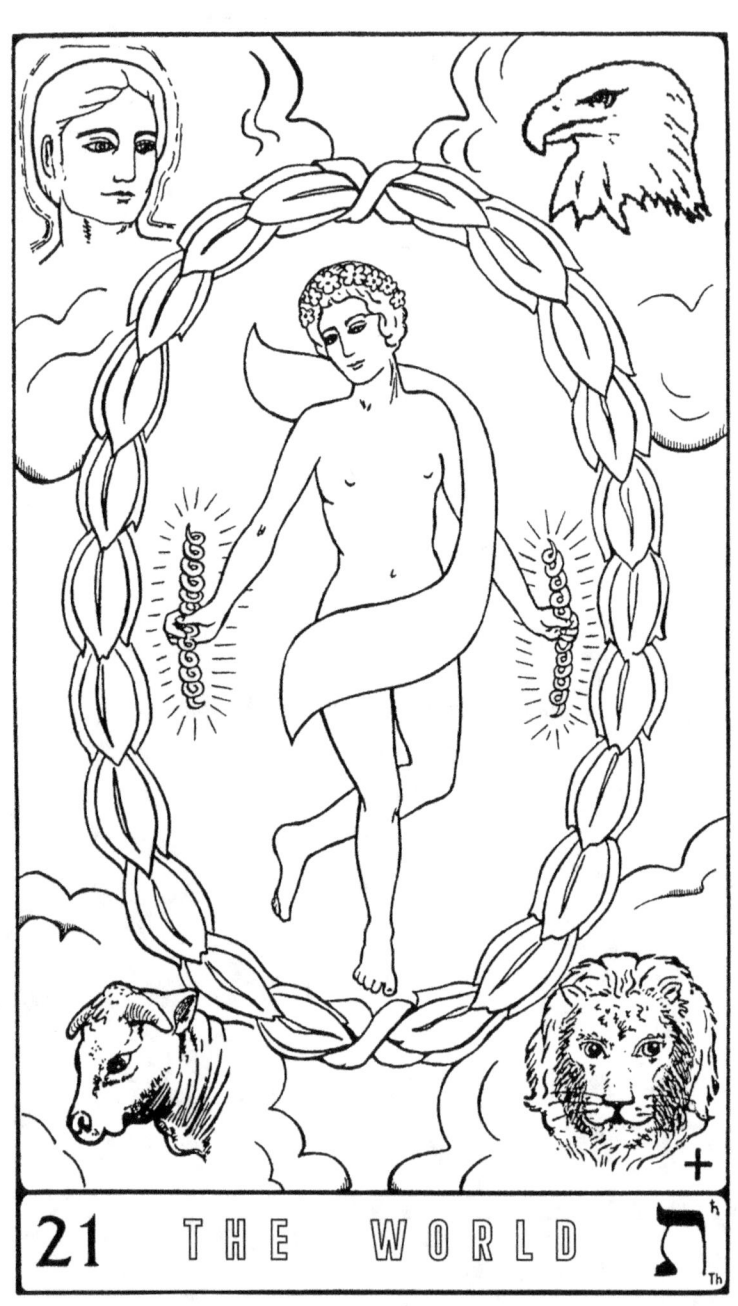

The World
21

Tav

Key Twenty-one: 21 is the final Key and letter. It is the Seventh Stage of Spiritual Unfoldment. Tav represents the element Earth, the Creation. Here that element reaches its ultimate. It is the goal of the Great Work.

Path of Wisdom 32 is called the Administrative Intelligence, sometimes the Assisting or Serving Intelligence, because "it directs all operations of the seven planets, with their divisions, and concurs therein."

Letter T, or Th: in Hebrew "Tav," means "cross," "mark," or "signature." This Key marks the signature at the culmination of the Major Arcana series. It is a letter signifying perfection, without any negative connotation.

The numerical value of the letter Tav is 400 in the Hebrew alphabet.

Identity: The inner secret of the cross is the Center where the One Identity has its Abode. This is the Palace of Holiness in the midst, where the Ruling Principle dwells.

Function: The function of this Key is Cosmic Consciousness. The Greek word for "world" is Cosmos, as meaning the whole universe.

Astrologically: Saturn rules this Key. The limitation and discipline which led to this point have their reward. Concentration is also an act of limitation.

SYMBOLOGY OF THE COLORS AND ELEMENTS

The central point is a positive reality, the Place of God; yet it is that which is not, because without form or dimension—hence "is not."

He who finds the Self finds the World-Ruler.

In the four corners of the picture are seen the same mystical figures as in Key 10 The Wheel of Fortune, except here the bull is turned away from the lion and from the center, to indicate forces moving out toward concrete manifestation.

The four animals represent the fixed signs and elements of the zodiac, and the fixed conditions in which all manifestation takes place. Also the Great Name IHVH, or Tetragrammaton.

The wreath is an ellipse, a zero-sign, resting above the figures of those creatures representing Earth and Fire, that is, the bull and the lion, because man's power of giving form to fiery energy helps him weave together the leaves.

The 22 leaves represent the 22 modes of force derived from that One Energy, each leaf in three parts to denote the three modes of the Life-Power's expression—Integrative, Disintegrative, and Equilibrating. They are the 22 letters of the living Word.

The dancer is the celestial androgyne, both male and female. She/he is the embodiment of the fiery Life-Power. Her/his dance suggests the Law of Rhythm, at work everywhere, and the perfect balance of one who commands both her/his own vehicle and the elements.

She/he is more than would appear, as indicated by the veil which partially hides her/his figure.

The veil is shaped like Kaph, the letter of Key 10 The Wheel of Fortune, and is allotted the purple color associated with that Key, and its planet Jupiter. This suggests that the mechanism of the universe tends to conceal and draw attention away from the truth of Reality.

Two spirals in her/his hands turn in opposite directions—dual operations of the One Force, in integration and disintegration, complementary activities which are being carried on simultaneously, and without end, balancing each other.

Here the goal of the Great Work having been reached, the Father and Son have become One, and rule from the throne at the Center of Self. The personal self has become identified with the Central Reality of the universe. The three aspects of humanity in Key 20 Judgement have merged into one whole.

> *"God was in Christ, reconciling the World to Himself."*
> *(2 Corinthians 5:19)*

COLORING INSTRUCTIONS

Green:	Wreath, except crossed ribbons at either end.
Blue:	Background (leave blank white ellipses around spirals).
Brown:	Animals; lion is more tawny, a little yellow added.
White:	Clouds, gray on white. Paint white rays from elliptical area around spirals.
Blonde:	Beak of eagle; hair of man and of dancer.
Violet:	Veil of Kaph, around Dancer.
Red:	Wreath on head of Dancer; X on ribbons at top and bottom of large oval wreath.

The color of Path 32 on the Tree of Life is blue-violet.

MEDITATION

I am Tav, the Mark or Signature,
Quintessence of the Perfected Work,
Poised among the elements of form.
Though held by none, I grasp
The forces that control them all.

Twenty-two leaves of my Sacred Book
Are woven in a ring, and set to frame
An open door unto the realm within
That calls the Wise and True.
And like the spiral, I begin anew.

The Twenty-Two Keys—The World: Key 21

The Tarot Tableau

The Tarot Tableau as a Lightning Flash

Many new facets will appear as you study the relationships between Keys in this chart. First, the Fool is descending right down through the series, in the zig-zag form of a flash of lightning which emanates forth from Kether, the Crown, on the Tree of Life.

Spirit descends into matter and rises again to follow the cycles of the universe. Conscious mind in its turn descends and rises, as does the subconscious mind.

The Fool moves on an independent and greater cycle, passing through and binding the whole together, to rise once more to finer heights, and to begin an even greater adventure as he evolves.

"God created a reality out of No Thing, called the nonentity into existence and hewed colossal pillars from intangible Air." (This is quoted from the most ancient written Cabalistic work called the *Book of Formation*. Its teachings were handed down by word of mouth for an untraceable length of time before taking written form.)

"God let the letter Aleph predominate in original Air (Key 0). He let the letter Mem predominate in original Water (Key 12). He let the letter Shin predominate in original Fire (Key 20)." They are the three Mother Letters. Their interaction signify that Man uses his will to master his surrounding conditions.

The seven double letters "serve to signify the antithesis to which human life is exposed." These are Beth, Gimel, Daleth, Kaph, Peh, Resh, and Tav. They depict the seven pairs of opposite conditions in life. They are Life and Death, Peace and Misfortune, Wisdom and Folly, Wealth and Poverty, Beauty and Ugliness, Fruitfulness and Devastation, and Dominion and Slavery.

The twelve simple letters, "having been designed, established, combined, weighed and changed by God, He performed by them twelve constellations in the world." The letters are: Heh, Vav, Zain, Cheth, Teth, Yod, Lamed, Nun, Samekh, Ayin, Tzaddi, and Qoph, each standing for one sign of the zodiac. They also each stand for the attributes of sight, hearing, smell, speech, taste, coition, work, movement, wrath, mirth, meditation, and sleep. And, they also stand for the 12 months of the year.

Aleph and Tav (Keys 0 and 21) are the first and the last—the beginning and the perfected end of the Work. These are free of the pattern, for each represents perfection in a different way; each is so to speak "on a cloud," the one descending, the other ascending.

The Spirit and the Bride say, "COME."

When one becomes the Cosmos, he is ready to begin the Great Work of guiding others; let all seek to attain this state for:

MANY ARE ON THE PATH, BUT FEW HAVE SHOWN THE WAY.

www.ingramcontent.com/pod-product-compliance
Lightning Source LLC
Chambersburg PA
CBHW050028130526
44590CB00042B/2047